P9-DXM-634

D0037865

....
....
....
....
....

LET IT BANG

....
....
....
....
....

LET IT BANG

A Young

Black Man's

Reluctant

Odyssey

into Guns

RJ YOUNG

Houghton Mifflin Harcourt

BOSTON   NEW YORK

2018

Copyright © 2018 by RJ Young

All rights reserved

For information about permission to reproduce selections from this book, write
to trade.permissions@hmhco.com or to Permissions, Houghton Mifflin Harcourt
Publishing Company, 3 Park Avenue, 19th Floor, New York, New York 10016.

hmhco.com

Library of Congress Cataloging-in-Publication Data
Names: Young, R. J., (Writer), author.
Title: Let it bang : a young black man's reluctant odyssey into guns / R. J. Young.
Description: Boston : Houghton Mifflin Harcourt, 2018. |
Includes bibliographical references and index.
Identifiers: LCCN 2018012248 (print) | LCCN 2018035744 (ebook) |
ISBN 9781328826329 (ebook) | ISBN 9781328826336 (hardcover)
Subjects: LCSH: Young, R. J., (Writer) | African Americans — Social life and customs. |
Firearms — Social aspects — United States. | African Americans — Race relations. |
African American journalists — Biography. | LCGFT: Autobiographies.
Classification: LCC E185.86 (ebook) | LCC E185.86 .Y665 2018 (print) |
DDC 305.896/073 — dc23
LC record available at https://lccn.loc.gov/2018012248

Book design by Martha Kennedy

Printed in the United States of America
DOC 10 9 8 7 6 5 4 3 2 1

For Grandmomme

Of all creatures that breathe and move upon the earth, nothing is bred that is weaker than man.

— HOMER, *The Odyssey*

Guns are right up there with race as one of the most sensitive, taboo-ridden public issues we have. And the mystique gets bigger all the time.

— HENRY ALLEN, *"The Mystique of Guns"*

LET IT BANG

CONTENTS

1

CHARLES AND LIZZIE

WHEN I FIRST met Charles Stafford, it was simply in passing. I was at his house on a hill, one he could afford to have fenced, because my boss at the time, Mary, had invited me there to her son's high school graduation party. Mary's son had been a lifelong friend to Charles's son. The two were graduating together and throwing a party to celebrate in a place called Coweta.

Coweta is a town in Wagoner County, Oklahoma. It's the kind of place where the owner of a used-car lot thought he'd show his wit and charm by calling his business Shade Tree Cars and Trucks. It's the kind of town where a Shade Tree mechanic will pull over to find out why your car is broken down, fix the problem, and send you on your way, asking nothing more in return than a well-placed handshake. In Coweta, the word *shit* has four syllables, and you can still get popped in the mouth for saying it. It's also the kind of town where it's perfectly normal not to invite a single black person to a party.

I drove from my apartment in Tulsa out into the sticks, into *God's Country,* as I've heard it called, because Mary's secretary had instructed me that it was "a big deal" to be invited to one of Mary's family-related events. At the time, I was an intern for Mary at the University of Tulsa's Collins Fitness Center. To decline would not have been a good look, and could've led to a piss-poor work environment. So, because I had to, I found the place, pulled up, and stepped out of my piece-of-shit Oldsmobile Alero.

I stayed just long enough for my first-ever encounter with Charles's daughter, Lizzie. I could not avert my eyes from her. Lizzie wore a flowing lavender dress. Her hair was pulled back into a long, curly blonde ponytail that forced me to confront the ferocity and beauty of her features. She looked at me with the kind of contempt usually reserved for someone about to smash a puppy's head in with a brick. It took me a few seconds to realize I was *in her fucking seat.* I moved. She smiled then, and sat down.

I tried to mingle among the faces that looked nothing like mine, but I couldn't handle it. I found the nearest exit and left the place, which felt foreign and uncomfortable.

My story with Charles and Lizzie would've ended here if I had not egregiously failed an elective, a class called Philosophy of Art. That was the first falling domino that led me to Lizzie. As a student at the University of Tulsa, I worked as a mechanic at Pep Boys part-time and as a personal trainer when I could get clients. I ran the sixty meters, two hundred meters, and four hundred meters — all really fucking slowly — for the track team, and was a member of the co-ed cheerleading squad. You might find it funny that the little scholarship money I did receive came from cheerleading. Or, as I was fond of saying, throwing white girls in the air.

I'd signed up for the philosophy class to fulfill a requirement for my degree in exercise and sports science, but signing up was pretty much all I did. The loud thud of the F, when it landed on my up-till-then pretty damn good GPA, meant I was in danger of being placed on academic probation, while being still three hours short of the 124 hours I needed to finish my degree. And I had no money for summer school.

Yes, I'd slipped when I failed Philosophy of Art. I was tired and not much interested in what dead white men like Immanuel Kant and Georg Hegel had to say about anything, let alone the meaning of life. And it had been only six months since a member of the financial aid department at TU looked me square in the eye while saying, "If you can't afford to be here, then you shouldn't be here." This after carrying loans that surely will be hanging over my head long after global warming has become global scorched earth. So, I was overjoyed when Mary offered me a paying job at the fitness center through the summer.

TAKING THE JOB with Mary came with one caveat. She'd asked that I consent to work as a trainer with her friend's daughter.

"Can I meet her first?" I said.

"You've met her."

"I have? Who is she?"

"She'll be here tomorrow. I expect you to be here too."

When I showed up at work the next day, I saw Mary standing beside the woman who had told me with nothing more than a furrowed brow and a twitch of the nose that I was *in her fucking seat*. She was looking back at me.

The toughest part of working out with someone who doesn't want to work out is finding something to talk about. But with Lizzie there was no talking. Well, there was, but it was decidedly one-sided and repetitive. I would ask a question, and she would either roll her eyes or raise her eyebrows. Rather than attempt an exercise I asked her to try, she would just stare. This went on for a few days, until I asked her if she would rather just walk the track. In response, she simply turned and began walking up the stairs to the second level of the facility, where the track was. Just being with me for an hour, in a place that looked built to torture her physically and emotionally, was horrible for Lizzie. She'd been overweight for most of her life and was somewhat resigned to that. I would try to empathize with her. But nobody wants to hear how the currently fit trainer was once a fat kid. Mary knew this about my background, and it was why she chose to bring Lizzie and me together. Even though it wasn't working, I continued to try to relate to Lizzie.

This was our routine for about a week. Because after

most of my sessions with Lizzie, I also trained Mary, along with Lizzie's mother, Nancy, they'd ask how things were going with Lizzie, and I was fine with telling them. That is, until the day I lost my temper with Lizzie and, straight to her face, called her "kind of a bitch." She didn't speak to me after I said those words to her. She simply gave me the finger and walked away. I knew then that I would be fired.

Except I wasn't.

Mary and Nancy told me that this white girl's getting pissed off and flipping me the bird was a good thing. That I had elicited emotion from Lizzie, which was precisely what they'd hoped for when putting the black man who talked too much together with the white woman who talked little to not at all. No, they said, you're doing a good job. I've never thought two white women crazier than I did that day. The next day Lizzie showed up, which was cause enough for celebration. But then she said something.

"It's that you don't read," she said.

"What?"

She did that furrowed-brow, nose-twitch thing again. "I don't expect someone like you to read."

"Someone like me?"

She gestured at my muscle shirt and shorts.

"Ah, I see," I said. "So you'd be surprised if I said I like Shakespeare."

She rolled her eyes. "No, you don't."

"'My words fly up, my thoughts remain below: Words without thoughts never to heaven go.'"

"Do it again," she said.

That was the first time I saw her winged smile. The one that quivers and disappears all at once, like the wings of a hummingbird. This is how the formal courtship began — with talking. We talked throughout all of our sessions after that one. But soon that hour proved to be insufficient. We talked through text messages — about books, about politics, about each other. Lizzie became the person I wanted to speak with each morning and the person I wanted to speak with before bed that night. She was my best friend, and I was grateful to be hers. And then she'd smile at me, and I no longer wanted to be just her friend. I wanted to be her most intimate friend too — her husband. I loved her. I never expected that to change, and it hasn't.

I eventually asked Lizzie to marry me. And she said yes. Because I loved Lizzie, I felt compelled to try to know her family. But by the first time Lizzie took me home to meet her parents, three months after we began dating, I knew just one thing about Charles, her father. The only thing he and I had in common was a mutual admiration for Lizzie.

CHARLES SHOOK MY hand the first time we formally met. Then he promptly left the room. Neither Lizzie nor Nancy found it alarming that he came back in with the biggest goddamn revolver I'd ever seen. They didn't think it was weird that he would hand it to me either. I felt certain that I had landed in either Wes Craven's rendition of *Guess Who's Coming to Dinner* or the next film in the *Saw* franchise. I knew that in a horror movie, the black man usually dies first. I was waiting for one of the three white people in the room to tell me how most people are so ungrateful to be alive, or how they would've voted for Obama a third time — right before performing a lobotomy on me in the family den.

Charles pointed to the gun in my hand. "It's a Judge." I didn't know what that meant, and I don't think he knew what it meant to hand me, a young black man, a revolver that Dirty Harry would be scared of. Once the feeling of fright dimmed, the absurdity of this event hit me. To show me what a *down brotha* he was, the man wanted me to hold a pistol he could cross-load with .45 Long Colt and .410 shotgun shells?

As I got to know him, I would come to see this gesture as one of the Charles-est things ever. It was truly a display of friendship. But that day all I took in was how important firearms were to the man whose daughter I was dating. It was also my first clue as to how hard it was going to be to fit into his family.

AFTER CHARLES PLACED that cartoonish revolver in my hands, I made several other forays into the wilderness of Lizzie's family. The first came a year into our relationship, when she brought me, her boyfriend, home for Thanksgiving.

Nancy was smart enough to assume that her daughter and I might be sleeping in the same bed — which I would neither confirm nor deny. She told Lizzie it would be perfectly fine with both her and Charles if we chose to sleep in Lizzie's bed. Two feet from her parents' bedroom. Pass.

I think Nancy knew I would say no because she'd already turned down the bed in the guest room for me, and that's where I slept that night. The next day I woke, and drove to the gym in town for a lift and a run. I came back to the house to find a set of Round House overalls, gray long johns, white socks, brown gloves, and a heavy brown Carhartt jacket, with a pair of work boots on the floor. I turned to look at Lizzie.

"I hope they fit," she said.

I checked the tags and the size of the boots. They did. "But what do I need them for?"

At this Lizzie merely smiled and handed me a wool cap. "He's waiting on you."

"Waiting on —"

Charles burst into the room. "Come on, RJ. Get changed. We got work to do."

Before I had the chance to ask what I was getting changed for, Lizzie and Charles left the room and closed the door. This left me with no option except to put on the clothes. Then I walked outside, and the biting wind hit me head on, making a cold day colder than Ice Cube's *No Vaseline*. Lizzie's younger brother, Jimmy, who would be my future brother-in-law, and Charles were waiting for me. They told me it was time to get in the truck. I could see my breath, and yet my hands were beginning to sweat inside the gloves. What on earth was I doing with these white men?

Charles drove up to the gate that separated the five acres his house was built on from the rest of his property. Jimmy stepped out of the truck and unlocked the padlock on the large green metal gate. He swung it wide, and Charles drove through. After Jimmy closed the gate, we drove up and over a hill. On the descent, I could make out what looked like a small orange metal corral connected to a blue metal chute. As we drew closer, another truck pulled up, and out popped two more men. The three of us stepped out of our truck, and I was introduced to Charles's brother-in-law, Jay, and his son, Mikey, who lived on the hill just across the pasture. Through this introduction and the following conversation, I came to understand just what the hell we were doing out on a biting-cold, gray November day, when even the sun knew better than to come out and play. We were going to vaccinate cows.

But to vaccinate cows, you need cows. And to get the cows you need to round them up. So Mikey and Charles each jumped back into a truck and began herding cattle toward the corral. Soon those animals were milling about in the pen, sounding terrified. I was just standing there, feeling like an idiot. Jimmy held out two long black sticks, indicating I was supposed to pick one up. I noticed their ends looked different.

I cagily took one from his hands. "What's this?"

"It's a bull whip."

"What do you have?"

He hit a button at the top of the stick's grip, and a fierce wave of lightning flashed.

"An electric cattle prod?"

Jimmy's face took on an *Ain't it cool?* expression, and I started to do the only thing I could think of: use my phone to record what was happening. Outside my comfort zone, all but paralyzed by the absurdity of watching cows with *horns* being crammed into the pen. Of thinking how the smell of a newly pinched cow turd punishes your nose for simply performing its natural function, while Charles showed how impressed he was with the size of the heifer's stool.

"Boy, they're shitting good!"

He said it with ferocious pride, like a newborn's father cooing through the glass at the hospital nursery. Of course, this is Charles's livelihood. This is how he feeds his family; to him, cattle are an important commodity. But for me, this was all new. I was trying to survive this initiation into Lizzie's family.

Mikey ushered each cow individually into the blue chute and into a neck brace. Then Charles and Jay took turns sticking a cow in the neck with a needle filled with a one-stop-shop vaccination. The process looked barbaric to me. But I eventually became sort of enchanted, watching those cows and calves taking offense at being manhandled. I was happy as a voyeur, but that role was not to last. One large cow balked at entering the chute, and I was handed the electric cattle prod.

"Juice him, RJ!"

Which was Charles trying to help me do something useful, rather than fiddling with my phone and playing dress-up. Despite my reservations, I poked the cow. I was frightened to see it rear up on its hind legs and get *pissed*. Then I realized that it wasn't a cow at all. It was a bull. I still don't know how my shorts remained unsoiled.

After about three hours, more than 120 cows had been penned, slammed down the chute, and boosted with vaccinations. Mikey celebrated with a soda and inadvertently spilled a bit on Jay's truck.

"I'm sorry," I said. I was only vaguely aware that I didn't owe Mikey an apology for the fact that he'd spilled his own damn soda. I was basically past logical thought processes by then.

"Forget it," Mikey said. "It's a Toyota anyway."

2

WE'RE ALL MAD HERE

BEFORE I'D BEGUN to court Charles's firstborn, I had little desire to know about guns because I believed I knew enough about them already. Which is to say, I knew that a gun, especially in the hands of a complete stranger with a badge and a mandate to protect and serve, could get me killed.

For the first twelve years of my life, my family lived in Hattiesburg, Mississippi, and Panama City, Florida, cities in the South where firearms are plentiful. Yet we didn't have anything to do with guns.

Although my father did look forward to watching new episodes and, in some cases, reruns of the reality TV show *COPS*. He'd even sit through the commercials rather than risk missing anything. *COPS* is police-procedural porn that frequently focuses on poor people in poor neighborhoods. That's exactly the focus that the audience wants. In 2011, *COPS* became the longest-running show in the history of the Fox Broadcasting Company. At the time, its only real competition for that honor was *America's Most Wanted*, another show focusing on the worst of us — fugitives from the law who have committed serious and heinous crimes. But my father's impulse to watch *COPS* wasn't based on the desire to watch as the dregs of society get their comeuppance. It was something else. "We need to know what they're doing now," he'd say.

By "they" my father meant beat cops in blue driving around in a squad car, locked, loaded, and looking for action. As municipal police in different parts of the country discussed what they were expecting might occur, a cameraman — who I hope received some sort of hazard pay — rode along and shot the action as the cops chased a suspect, apprehended that suspect, and placed him under arrest. My father took lessons from this show, and he'd share them with me. "There's very little difference between a cop and psycho when they've got a gun. Both of them want to pull their gun on you. So don't let them search your car. They'll plant things there and say it was there *the whole time*. The law is on their side *all the time*. You're at the mercy of a psycho who is permanently on the side of the law. That's scary, son. You're right to be scared. And *COPS* teaches you that."

My father said this frequently. He meant that, as a black man, it was incumbent upon me to know and understand the tactics police use to corner, intimidate, and incriminate black men. When I was fourteen, one in six black men in my

country had ended up in prison. A year later, while standing on the sidewalk outside the Springdale Shopping Center
in North Tulsa, a white cop bombarded me with questions
about why I was there. I could see he wasn't sure if I was
telling the truth about shopping at a clothing store called
Tops & Bottoms, but then he noticed the academy-style Eagle Scout ring on my finger. He smiled. "That ring just saved
you a trip to the pokey, son." This was not the first time I'd
been interrogated on the street about who I was and what I
was doing at a certain place. That this cop could see a pudgy
five-foot-five black kid with a peach-fuzz mustache as a
threat — as an adult — frightened me then, and it frightens
me now. That we live in a nation where blacks, who make
up just 13 percent of the US population, make up nearly 40
goddamn percent of the prison population is fairly common
knowledge. But to me, every day was and is a struggle not
to become one of these statistics. Every day I am afraid of it.

These are facts my parents knew. They sought to prepare
me, in the best way they could, to live in a country full of
people who think less of me, or think I might do them harm,
because my skin is brown and my hair is dark and curly. I
believed that my wielding of a gun would only serve to give
these people more reason to act on what they already believed. So I made a point to avoid guns whenever I could,
wherever I could.

IT TOOK SOME time for me to get used to seeing a shotgun leaning against the side door every time I walked into

Charles's house. Cold and black, the gun stood watch in case of intruders. I took note of the alarm-system keypad just across the room and contemplated the security overkill. But the side-door shotgun was not the only gun Charles kept in plain view. It was not uncommon to find a pistol or revolver lying on the kitchen table, along with a half-empty box of shells. Lizzie told me this was normal in Charles's house and not meant to intimidate or scare me. But it did scare me. Charles owned small handguns, large handguns, handguns with cylinders like those that nineteenth-century US marshals used, handguns like the ones modern police use. Charles didn't come to own assault rifles until he was in his sixties. But handguns? Charles has owned handguns for most of his life.

On one occasion, I asked about his self-defense sidearm: a gun I'd seen him stick in a bag like an oversized wallet that he carried.

"Why do you carry that gun?" I asked. "And why do you have so many?"

Charles, sitting in his favored recliner, took a deep breath and said something about needing to go down to the wrecker shop. He made for the door, only briefly slowing down to pick up his jacket and hat, and left me alone in the living room. A few minutes later Lizzie emerged from her bedroom.

"Where'd he go?" she asked.

"He said he was going to the wrecker shop, but I think I made him mad."

"What? How?"

"I just asked him why so many guns."

"Oh, baby." She took on a defeated look and then sat down across from me. That was when I learned from Lizzie that you don't comment on how many guns a person has. You don't ask how many guns they've bought. You don't ask how many guns they've sold. "It's like asking how much money you make, or how many times a week you have sex with your wife," Lizzie said. "You just don't do it."

Charles interpreted my questions the way a corner boy might, though he stopped short of giving me side eye and asking, *Nigga, is you wearing a wire?*

My parents taught me there is no such thing as a stupid question, but clearly they were wrong. I felt embarrassed about the whole thing. I wasn't keen on learning about guns in the first place, and now I'd been made to feel like a fool for what I didn't know. *Fuck it.* This old man was not proving to be worth the effort, and I was tired of pushing. So I stopped. Until he gave me reason not to.

SOON AFTER VACCINATION Thanksgiving, despite my best efforts and mechanical know-how, my Alero finally decided to depart this weary world. It died in its sleep. I had parked it outside the apartment that Lizzie and I now pretty much shared, and the car refused even to cough a start the next morning. I checked the battery. I tested the spark plugs, and I tested the alternator, and when those things failed, I went to the obvious. Did the car have gas? Was I using the correct key? Was I even in the right car? After more than a day of tinkering and phone calls to auto-tech friends much smarter than me, I gave up. The car was dead, and I needed to start walking. When I arrived home that night, Lizzie met me at the door and held out a key she'd made. It was for her Impala.

"We can share," she said.

This was no small gift in a state where public transportation is for shit, and it is nearly impossible to get from one place to another without four wheels and a driver's license. Lizzie and I shared her car for several months, and that's when it became clear to me that though she held down a job that covered her rent, her parents were paying for her degree in English literature as well as her car. I was unaccustomed to such acts of generosity. I'd never personally met anyone with the means and will to perform them. The weight of this discovery was jarring.

THE SCHISM IN my own family had begun purely because of finances, but religion and politics had strained things even further and made a relationship with my parents untenable. But I still needed family. Now that I was sharing Lizzie's car, the last thing I wanted her father to think was that I might be using her. On the next trip to Coweta, I waited until I could get Charles alone. It was two days before I caught him by himself at the kitchen table, reading the paper. I took a seat next to him, and then a deep breath.

"Charles?"

He took his time as if finishing a paragraph, laid the paper down, and peered at me over the top of his glasses. "RJ?"

"I realize you do a lot for Lizzie. But I want you to know that what you do for her is not what you do for me. I've made my own way, and I plan to continue doing that as long as Lizzie keeps me around."

Charles studied me for just a moment with a quizzical expression. "Does this mean you're not going to let me buy you a car?"

See that? Just when I thought the old bastard was going to make it easy for me to continue to see him as a flat character in the rolling sitcom that is my life, he rounded out into the kind of person he'd raised his daughter to be: capable of great kindness and generosity. I didn't ask why. I just fought back tears and hugged him. Charles bought me my first truck that same weekend.

I resolved then to begin my quest to get to know Charles through what he liked best. I'd exhaust all avenues at my disposal until I felt comfortable enough to engage him on the topic of guns. This time I planned to do it right. I would avoid putting my foot in my mouth and keep quiet until I knew what questions to ask and in what manner to ask them.

I came close to derailment at Christmas. We opened our presents in Charles's house. He pretended to be a fat white man in a red suit, with a deer fetish, living in subzero temperatures most of the year, who had brought trinkets to each of us. But my eyes kept drifting back to the weapon of war on the floor next to Charles. For Christmas he had bought *himself* a Smith and Wesson AR-15 derivative. I didn't ask how he could just walk into Atwoods, the local farm-and-ranch-supply chain store, buy the thing off the shelf like a loaf of bread, and own it without fear. I kept that to myself. But just being in the same room with it felt crazy. This was *Christmas*. It was the day of good cheer, bad music, and ugly sweaters; of whimsy, of family, of fun. But I had none until Charles finally took this rifle, which had been banned by law throughout most of my life, back to his bedroom. I kept that to myself too.

But that Christmas I wondered how my country had gotten to be so over-the-top demanding about the right to bear arms — the biggest, baddest arms we can get our hands on. Why do so many adults I know, not just in Coweta, but across Oklahoma and the entire country, think they need a gun? Our nation hasn't fought a war on its own soil since December 7, 1941, and before that, 1861, when the country picked a fight with itself. So, what war were the people — *white people* — in my life preparing for? All too quickly I began to feel like a little blond girl in a pinafore stuck at the bottom of a rabbit hole.

> *"But I don't want to go among mad people," Alice remarked.*
>
> *"Oh, you can't help that," said the Cat: "we're all mad here. I'm mad. You're mad."*

"How do you know I'm mad?" Alice said.

"You must be," said the Cat, "or you wouldn't have come here."

I was thinking, Quite, Cat. Quite.

SINCE I DIDN'T know anyone trustworthy who could teach me about gun culture, this quest began privately. I started my education with what I could easily get my hands on — music. I was amazed at how much gun culture had seeped into me already from this source. Machine-gun fire and loud pistol popping percussed the music I grew up listening to — it was just part of the track. 50 Cent had already conditioned me to the names AK-47 and AR-15 as normal parts of a conversation. I knew about night vision, shell catchers, and infrared beams, and that 50 Cent keeps a gun big enough to intimidate Shaq. (Never mind that a gun as small as a pocket pistol would likely intimidate Shaq because Shaq is not a stupid man.)

Wu-Tang Clan told me how the *gun will go*. The music I listened to taught me that Uzis, MAC-10s, and M16A2s were *choppas*. Mobb Deep told me *survival of the fittest* means being strapped with a gun and ready to die using it. Lil Wayne told me that to *do my thang* included shooting a person with a Glock, not to kill, but to render comatose. Ludacris told me that saying *we got* with a hard edge was meant to be heard as *we got guns*. N.W.A. told me coming *Straight Outta Compton* also meant leaving with a sawed-off shotgun in hand. As a teenager, I was intrigued with the heft of lethal force, what it meant to hold that shit in your hands, to focus rage and anger into a single trigger squeeze.

One day, I found myself riding with Charles in his truck, and he began singing along to a country song. I brought up the idea that country music is just as bad as rap music in its characterization of violence. That it was just as bad as hip-hop in its depiction of women as objects, and to act as if that statement wasn't true was the sort of exercise in arrogance that black people weren't allowed.

"You just don't like George Strait," Charles said.

Perhaps, but why is it considered crude and inflammatory for ASAP Ferg to rap about his violent, psychotic uncle carrying his grandmother's kitchen knives and that same grandmother hiding a gun from the uncle under her pillow in "Let It Bang," but endearing and downright quaint for Aaron Lewis to write a country song about his grandfather's shotgun and how it was used to back down burglars and shoot up road signs in "Granddaddy's Gun"? When white men use six strings and G-chords to write songs about their fascination with guns as a means of protection for and pride in their families, they are raised up as symbols of good family men, willing and able husbands, brothers, and sons. But let a black man write a song about how he uses a gun to stake a claim, to stand his ground, to negotiate business — much as many lauded political and military leaders have done throughout history — and watch that black man be made out to be a criminal, whether or not he has committed an actual crime.

The idea endures that country music is based on wholesome values, but studies are finding otherwise. Country and rap lyrics, once you peel away the cultural differences, have generally similar violent through-lines. (What's more, country music actually makes more references to drugs than any other major musical genre, while rap makes the fewest.) And yet the band plays on — another system that rewards white men for brandishing firearms in art and life while crushing black men who do, for any reason.

Which doesn't make music any different than cinema. On film, white men oozing with armed-up machismo abound, from westerns to sci-fi to action blockbusters.

It's impossible to make an action movie without machine guns, submachine guns, and fully automatic weapons, for fear of seeming lame. Yet how many black action stars can you come up with? In his Oscar-winning role as Alonzo Harris in *Training Day,* Denzel Washington drops to the floor for a shotgun to shoot at — and just miss — his new partner, Jake Hoyt (Ethan Hawke). Jake runs away but is cornered in a kitchen and stalked by Alonzo, a black man with a shotgun, a black man toying with his white prey: "You know I'm surgical with this bitch, Jake. How you want it, dawg? Closed-casket?" And there it was: my visceral first experience of seeing a black man holding power over a white man. I was fourteen when Alonzo became an example of just how I didn't have to take this shit anymore. He was the man allowed to leave this world on his own terms (even if those terms included being gunned down by white members of the mafia) because he set those terms. He was a black man for whom the rules were whatever he said they were. Because he had a gun.

I had little idea of the differences between revolvers, semiautomatic pistols, and fully automatic weapons, or their history, until I stumbled upon a film called *Lord of War*. The movie is told from the vantage point of an illegal arms dealer named Yuri Orlov; it took me far into understanding the wider world of guns. Yuri's voice-over discussed the AK-47:

> *"Of all the weapons in the vast Soviet arsenal, nothing was more profitable than Avtomat Kalasnikova model of 1947, more commonly known as the AK-47, or Kalashnikov. It's the world's most popular assault rifle, a weapon all fighters love. An elegantly simple nine-pound amalgamation of forged steel and plywood, it doesn't break, jam, or overheat. It will shoot whether it's covered in mud or filled with sand. It's so easy even a child could use it, and they do. The Soviets put the gun on a coin. Mozambique put it on their flag. Since the end of the Cold War, the Kalashnikov has become the Russian people's greatest export. After that comes vodka, caviar, suicidal novelists."*

I stopped the movie and rewound it to hear this monologue again. *Wait,* I thought. That part about the AK-47 being Russia's greatest export can't be true. But Yuri was closer to the truth than most people think.

Then there's my favorite literary reference to the feeling of holding and using a gun, a paragraph-length soliloquy of a sentence in *Billy Bathgate*, which E. L. Doctorow couldn't bring himself to punctuate with anything other than commas.

> *I will never forget how it felt to hold a loaded gun for the first time and lift it and fire it, the scare of its animate kick up the bone of your arm, you are empowered there is no question about it, it is an investiture, like knighthood, and even though you didn't invent it or design it or tool it the credit is yours because it is in your hand, you don't even have to know how it works, the credit is all yours, with the slightest squeeze of your finger a hole appears in a piece of paper sixty feet away, and how can you not be impressed with yourself, how can you not love this coiled and sprung causation, I was awed, I was thrilled, the thing is guns come alive when you fire them, they move, I hadn't realized that.*

This beautiful run-on sentence let me in on the psychological underpinnings of the fascination with guns, but it also illuminated a glaring lack in my knowledge of them. To know a gun, I'd have to own one. To know Charles, I'd have to shoot one.

3

GLOCK

IN HIS TRUCK, in traffic, Charles could become flustered while speaking on his mobile phone — a flip phone that might have come straight out of Captain Jean-Luc Picard's hand in 2000. Charles doesn't use it to text, play Words with Friends, scroll through Instagram, or check Facebook. In fact, if you text Charles, it could quite literally be *months* before you get a response, and only after his son or daughter had helped him clear the cobwebs from this digital relic. However, if you call him, he's going to answer. Or he's going to call you right back. The conversation might be short, but it will most certainly be had.

Therefore, it surprised none of us — Lizzie, Jimmy, and me — to hear that Charles had been talking on his phone and not giving his undivided attention to the road ahead. That makes him like almost anybody else with a mobile phone, four wheels, and a steering wheel, of course. The rub came when the fella in front of him jumped out of his ve-

hicle at a stoplight and started waving his hands and shouting, "Get off your phone! Get off your phone!"

From a white man's perspective, this was unusual, a little
surreal. As a black man, I would've taken it as a fairly common part of life; a white man shouting demands at me is at
the same time nothing new and an adrenaline-pumping po-
tential crisis.

Then Charles said, "I had to put that gun underneath my
leg." This time it was the .38 snub-nose revolver that he kept
in a small purse, along with his wallet and keys. Turns out
Charles's truck gun — the one you leave in the truck not because it's cool or collectible but because when you need to do
a job, that sumbitch will get her done — was a .38 snub-nose.
I realized then he didn't mean to tell this tale to be funny so
much as to convey that he'd felt threatened and that reaching
for a handgun in that instant made all the sense in the world.

CHASMS STILL EXISTED between Charles and me, and
I was still determined to use guns to bridge them. Charles's
gun of choice was a revolver. He respected the Glock enough
to pick one up when he needed a semiautomatic for absolute certainty that his gun would fire. But, given a choice, he
preferred a revolver. "Doesn't jam," he said. I wasn't interested in revolvers, though, except to know how they func-
tioned and how, in the evolution of guns, revolvers had led
to the advent of semiautomatic pistols. A revolver is the
kind of handgun John Wayne carried.

The handgun that captured my attention was the Glock.

All over the country, this gun appears in silhouette on the doors of movie theaters, restaurants, and almost all government offices as the symbol on the sign that says NO GUNS. Glocks are layered over movies and literature. In *The Fugitive*, Tommy Lee Jones plays the US marshal Sam Gerard, who tells Robert Downey Jr., playing special agent John Royce, "Get yourself a Glock and lose that nickel-plated sissy pistol." Having a little fun with the white-machismo-oozing protagonist who pollutes Hollywood action movies is Will Smith, who, as Detective Mike Lowry, throws off his Klan bed sheet, points dual two-tone Glock 17s at criminals, and yells, "Blue power, motherfuckers! Miami PD!" That's just the kind of scene that makes an impression on a sixteen-year-old black kid in Oklahoma.

AFTER THREE DECADES in manufacturing, Gaston Glock saw his opportunity. By the early 1980s, he'd worked his way into a contract to make knives and bayonets for his native Austria, and had spent considerable time around the decision makers at Austria's Ministry of Defense. There, he learned that the military needed a new sidearm, something to replace the Walther P-38, by then a relic of World War II. Officials literally laughed at him when he requested permission to enter the bidding for the pistol contract, and for good reason. Who the hell was he then, but a railroad worker's son with a metal shop? The ministry heads could not imagine that designing a gun from scratch was in his repertoire, but they didn't say no.

Glock immersed himself in pistols, including the Walther P-38. He examined its mechanics. He traveled back and forth to the country's patent office to learn more about the inner workings of pistols and the changes he would need to make. He sat down with members of the country's military establishment and learned from one Colonel Friedrich Dechant exactly what kind of pistol he envisioned — one that could "withstand extended contact with snow, ice, and mud," according to Paul Barrett, in his excellent history of the Glock. Furthermore, "it should fire ten thousand rounds with no more than one failure per thousand. The figure 40,000 was recorded that evening, referring to the goal that the ideal pistol should have a long service life, of forty thousand rounds."

Fourteen months after asking to enter the Austrian government's bidding process, Glock filed his first pistol patent. He called his pistol the Glock 17. It was his seventeenth invention. The Glock 17 magazine could hold up to seventeen rounds. As with the other pistols tested during bidding, the Glock 17 was shot ten thousand times. It failed to fire exactly once. In late 1983, the Austrian government bought twenty thousand of Glock's pistols.

IN THE UNITED States, it started with a 1984 magazine piece. Well, a gun-magazine piece, which is a great vehicle for ensuring that one hand washes the other if you're a gun manufacturer. When *Soldier of Fortune's* technical editor, Peter G. Kokalis, was told he could be the first gun writer in America to shoot a Glock 17, he couldn't wait to pull the trigger — pun very much intended. "Five thousand miles [to Austria] is a long way to travel just to shoot another 9 mm pistol," he wrote in the October 1984 issue. "But the Glock 17 is not just another pistol." He didn't hide how smitten he was: "Safe, reliable, accurate, instantly ready, easy to maintain, a minimal number of parts, light, compact, durable (almost indestructible), low felt recoil, a large capacity magazine, simplified training, and natural, instinctive pointing qualities — the Glock 17 possesses every single characteristic anyone has ever dreamed of having in a combat pistol."

His only real criticism, in this feature adding up to more than two thousand words, was that the Glock was not available for purchase in the United States. Truth is, it wasn't available to civilians anywhere. But by the time Kokalis's article appeared, members of the US Department of Defense were already considering it for military use. Folks in the Secret Service were given a few Glocks while in Vienna in 1985. As the gun was quietly making the rounds among folks in Washington, Gaston Glock and his lieutenants were setting up Glock Inc. in Smyrna, Georgia, just north of Atlanta. This while the gun was being introduced to a veritable who's who of international leaders, including Hafez Al-Assad, the father of the current Syrian president, Bashar Al-Assad, as well as Muammar Gaddafi in Libya. It was catching the interest of virtually every world leader with an army. And that's when the proverbial shit hit the proverbial fan.

In January 1986, the *Washington Post* ran this headline over the columnist Jack Anderson's byline: GADDAFI
BUYING AUSTRIAN PLASTIC PISTOLS. Anderson reported that Gaddafi had bought a hundred Glocks and was
planning to arm terrorists with them. Gaston Glock refuted
this piece of information, and so did high-ranking employees in his company. But it was clear that Gaddafi surrogates
had visited Glock's operation in Deutsch-Wagram, Austria, where the pistols were manufactured. The *New York
Times* ran an editorial a month later, with the headline HI-
JACKER'S SPECIAL, about how easily the gun might get
through airport security.

Time magazine surmised that the gun could give would-
be airline hijackers "an edge that officials are finding increasingly difficult to counter." This "edge" was an allusion
to the plastic parts of the gun — only the barrel was metal.
By May of that same year, congressional hearings were held
to ascertain how dangerous Glock handguns could be in the
hands of terrorists.

By 1988, the Associated Press spotted one on the hip of
then police commissioner Benjamin Ward. Many federal,
state, and local police forces were inquiring about samples
of the Glock 17. In some cases, after obtaining one for the
purpose of examining it, the recipient would send Glock a
check and keep the gun. That same year the *New York Post*
called it a "super gun." Articles about the Glock and the
handwringing that ensued among elected and appointed
officials amounted to the kind of publicity that a gun manu-

facturer could only dream of, and it did little to curtail sales of the gun on American soil when it made landfall in 1988. And that was before Gaston Glock and his compatriots started to aggressively recruit law-enforcement tastemakers and decision makers. At a time when most folks thought the Internet was a tennis term, gun enthusiasts were coming around to wanting a Glock — as the thinking goes, if somebody wants it banned, it must be good.

At this time, many police departments still issued revolvers. But firearms instructors were coming around to the Glock. Gun aficionados respected these instructors (as they still do), and once the instructors got past the ugly look of the gun, which is made of polymer where it *can* be and metal where it *has* to be, they began to see the advantages of the Glock 17. For starters, the Glock doesn't have a safety. This means it does not have to remain in a cocked position to be ready to fire at a moment's notice. At the time, the Colt 1911 was the most popular semiautomatic pistol. With this and other semiautomatics, accidental discharges were just a fact of life. Glocks are in this way like many revolvers; they don't have a safety. But one real advantage of a Glock was that it had fewer parts than most revolvers — by half. As a comparison, the Smith & Wesson 645 has more than a hundred parts. The Glock 17 has just thirty-four. You can literally take apart several different Glock 17s, jumble the parts, and reassemble the original number of guns. All of them will fire. This structure makes it much easier to maintain a Glock.

The Glock 17's most significant advantage becomes obvious when a shooter switches from squeezing off a revolver to squeezing off a Glock, especially for repeated rounds. In many cases, the hammer of a revolver remains de-cocked, which means the first squeeze must be especially forceful, but subsequent ones less so. But the hammer remains cocked for another blast after the initial round is fired. With a revolver the shooter must remember to use less force for the following shots. Most people, including members of law enforcement, don't practice enough with a revolver to know the amount of pressure they need to place on the trigger for the gun to fire. Indeed, one of the first lessons you learn about shooting a pistol is that when the gun fires, it should be a surprise to you — don't anticipate the recoil. Many people who shoot a revolver shoot low and then high, in many cases wasting two of a maximum of six rounds. With a Glock, the trigger pressure remains the same, whether it's the first shot, the second, or the seventeenth. That matters, particularly for law enforcement.

Also, in a firefight, the person with a Glock 17 has a three-to-one advantage over a shooter with a revolver, which has only six rounds of ammo. And yes, there's a myth that Glocks jam — Charles bought into that myth — but they don't do so regularly. Finding a Glock that jams is like finding a Toyota broken down on the side of the road.

The ease of use, of learning to be a good shot, comes easier with a Glock 17 because its recoil and return to target are fluid. You don't need to worry about smacking yourself in the nose because the caliber of bullet, the gun itself, or both, are just too powerful to control. The nine-millimeter rounds the Glock 17 fires are cheap and abundant. It's much easier, as we gamers say, to *Get good, son,* when you don't have to fight the equipment you're using or, more to the point, when it's not fighting you.

All of this led me to believe the Glock was the most efficient, easy-to-use pistol in the world. When I was finally ready, and told Charles I'd decided to get my own gun, and that I thought it should be a Glock, he thought about it for the length of time it takes to squeeze a trigger. He didn't ask me for my reasons. He didn't tell me I was wrong to want a Glock. He simply said, "We need to go to the gun show."

4

OBAMA AIN'T GONNA KNOW

AT FIRST I wondered why we needed to go to a gun show to buy a gun. After all, Charles lives about three miles from a store called Frank's Gun & Repair. It's at the corner of Highway 51 and 121st Street, just north of the Phillips 66 and across the street from the railroad tracks. Can't miss it. Can't mistake it, either, with its red-and-black-lettered sign spelling out 486-GUNS just below the word GUNS (again), in obstinate Republican red. Plus, Charles and the store owner, Frank, were downright social.

Indeed, Charles could buy, sell, or trade any one of the guns he owns there. I knew that Frank had recently serviced a handgun for Charles, after Charles had claimed that it wouldn't fire and was probably a piece of shit. Frank took a look at it. Cleaned it. Lubed it. Rubbed it down and had the pistol firing like new.

So I thought Frank's is where we'd go when I told Charles I had come around to the idea that I needed a Glock. But

I soon came to learn I'd given Charles too good a reason to do what many gun owners do for fun: go see what somebody else has got. Guns are apparently a lot like baseball cards. Folks are in love with their own collection, envious of somebody else's, and willing to shell out an obscene amount of money to get to brag about owning some rare specimen.

There's not a whole lot Charles will travel for. Only recently has Nancy convinced him that staying a night in Branson, Missouri, or Memphis, Tennessee, ain't gonna hurt him or the cattle. But if there's a gun show in Tahlequah, about an hour east of Coweta? Or if the Oklahoma Rifle Association is having a meeting in Oklahoma City? He'll set right out.

Finally, a couple years into my relationship with Lizzie, when we were engaged to be married, he'd begun to think of me as something like a son. That's what this trip was — a father and a son going to buy the son's first gun, at the world's largest gun show. Truth is, without Charles, I had about as much chance of walking into a gun show all by my lonesome as a Carnival Cruise liner would have docking in Antlers, Oklahoma.

IN OKLAHOMA, THERE'S a gun show almost every weekend of the year, which is right in line with the national trend. The Bureau of Alcohol, Tobacco, Firearms and Explosives estimates there are more than two thousand gun shows held in the United States annually. But the National

Association of Arms Show puts that figure closer to fifty-two hundred, or a hundred gun shows every weekend of the year.

Wanenmacher's Tulsa Arms Show occurs twice a year; the show organizer claims it is "the World's Largest Selection of antique, collector and modern firearms, knives, and accessories." Usually lasting a weekend, the Wanenmacher's show, located at the Tulsa Fairgrounds, covers eleven acres and boasts more than forty-two hundred tables and seven thousand vendors. Nearly forty thousand people visit the show on a given weekend. There's parking for RVs and scooters for rent.

The first gun show put on by Wanenmacher's was sponsored by the Indian Territory Gun Collectors Association in April 1955. A small group of avid enthusiasts met at a sportsman's sporting-goods store called, I shit you not, Sportsman Sporting Goods. It was located in what has become midtown Tulsa.

The idea of holding a show came about as a means to compare notes on what other gun collectors across the state had in their gun safes. When Joe Wanenmacher became club treasurer in 1968, he also took on the responsibility of organizing the semiannual gun show. In 1968 Wanenmacher counted 117 tables at the show. Then, President Lyndon B. Johnson signed the Gun Control Act of 1968. This act was the federal government's attempt to regulate the sale and transfer of firearms in the United States by requiring gun sellers to be licensed and by banning some small firearms. Attendance at the gun shows exploded the next year.

Two years in, Wanenmacher told the club he couldn't run the show for little to no payment anymore. That's when the club members asked him to take over the show permanently. The bargain was this: the show would retain the original club name, but all the profits would go into Wanenmacher's pocket. Eventually, the club name — Indian Territory Gun Collectors Association — gave way to a new one: Wanenmacher's. This was, perhaps, because the reference to the state's theft of territory from whole nations of people — which happened twice — felt awkward, but most likely, Wanenmacher just liked his own name. A petroleum engineer by trade, the man sensed he was about to strike oil.

Over the past forty-eight years, the show has achieved international acclaim because Wanenmacher willed it so. He traveled widely, recruiting collectors and salesmen from three continents and every state in the Union. The NRA's National Firearms Museum took a spot at a Wanenmacher's show in November 2014, to display guns owned by President Theodore Roosevelt and Annie Oakley. The actors Dan "Grizzly Adams" Haggerty and Lash LaRue have signed autographs at the show, as have members of the crew of the Enola Gay. According to Wanenmacher, the actor Tom Selleck once dropped by the show, in secret, to make a purchase. Fewer than 20 percent of collectors and salesmen at the show are Tulsans.

Wanenmacher also changed the direction of the show.

The Brady Handgun Violence Prevention Act went into effect in 1994. This law, supported by President Bill Clinton, banned semiautomatic weapons as well as high-capacity magazines. It also amended the Gun Control Act of 1968 to establish a five-day waiting period for unlicensed gun buyers. But, as with the passage of the Gun Control Act of 1968, the Brady Act of 1994 only brought more customers to Wanenmacher. Then the Federal Assault Weapons Ban expired in 2004. Four years later, a black man was elected president, and gun owners, mostly white ones, headed straight for the nearest gun show.

"Our good president probably has been the best gun salesman we've ever had, even better than Bill Clinton," Wanenmacher said in 2014. "I think . . . it's the fear of what he could do and knowing that we have a president who is the most anti-gun president we've ever had that motivated people to hoard even though now it looks like those things won't happen — at least not very soon."

CHARLES AND I visited Wanenmacher's show in November 2014, the year before the show turned sixty. Charles was dressed as he usually is. His polo shirt was tucked into his blue jeans, which he had pulled over the top of his cowboy boots. I was dressed as I usually am, in black hoodie, blue jumper jeans, and Jordan high-top sneakers. Charles took me around to the vendors, pointing out guns he thought were exciting or peculiar and stopping to chat with vendors whenever he felt gregarious. Whether my sense of vigilance was paranoia is debatable. I was painfully aware of how few black people I'd seen at the show. I didn't need all my fingers to count them.

A year after the founding of Black Lives Matter and two years after the killing of Trayvon Martin, it pained me and intrigued me to see the plethora of bumper stickers, T-shirts, and license plates with Confederate flags and dangerous rhetoric such as HERITAGE NOT HATE. One T-shirt I saw proclaimed this message: I JUST BOUGHT A NEW GLOCK, AND I CAN'T WAIT TO TRY IT OUT ON THE NEXT TRESPASSER.

Here's another: A GUN IN THE HAND IS BETTER THAN A COP ON THE PHONE.

And here's one more: GOD MADE MEN, BUT SAM COLT MADE THEM EQUAL.

The kind of people who buy those kinds of shirts made up the majority of people at the show, and I was decidedly not one of them.

We came to a vendor with a brand-new Glock 26 on display. "You want that one?" Charles asked. "I'll buy it." The Glock 26 is a subcompact, concealed-carry, nine-millimeter weapon affectionately known as the "Baby Glock." It's a pocket pistol specifically designed for self-defense. For that reason, the magazine holds just seven rounds, as opposed to the seventeen of other Glocks, and its grip is just long enough for an adult male to wrap three fingers around it.

The show features a list of twenty-one rules and guidelines. Among them is a warning to vendors: "You are urged, for your protection, to obtain and furnish identification for all sales." The state of Oklahoma does not require that background checks be performed on gun buyers, and that's as Wanenmacher wants it to be. Despite the fact that 92 percent of Americans favor background checks for all gun sales.

Charles knows that anybody who wants a gun will get a gun. But he's not afraid of a background check. He reached for his wallet to pay for the Glock. He was prepared to run this play the way the Bureau of Alcohol, Tobacco, Firearms and Explosives drew it up. He presented his I.D. and had a pen ready to fill out the Firearms Transaction Record for over-the-counter purchases. He was ready to allow the seller to give that information to the FBI, which would run it through the National Instant Criminal Background Check System, known as NICS.

The number of background checks performed by NICS has nearly doubled, from 11.2 million in 2007 to 21 million in 2015. Polls indicate that 14 million guns were sold from 2008 to 2011, while 20 million were sold from 2012 to 2013. Over 9 million guns were sold nationwide in 2015, according to the Bureau of Alcohol, Tobacco, Firearms and Explosives. But think of how many people don't report gun sales because they don't trust the government, journalists, or even nonpartisan polling and research institutions. And some states are slow to update even the data they do collect.

But when Charles offered to show the seller his driver's license, the seller waved away the gesture. "Obama ain't gonna know," he said. In fact, sellers have the right to waive this check, in accordance with the federal Firearm Own-ers' Protection Act of 1986, as long as they do not derive most of their income from selling guns. A number of states have, however, established laws making background checks mandatory for the purchase of any firearm at a gun show. But many more, including Oklahoma, may never join those states requiring this sort of vetting. So it did not matter that Charles was more than willing to abide by societal precau-tions meant to keep guns out of the hands of people who might do harm. The sellers themselves weren't.

Charles didn't seem the least bit fazed by what had oc-curred. He and I continued to walk through the gun show, having a look around. But I was keenly aware that I was carrying a Glock in a box, among people who, I knew well, could be armed, card-carrying members of the Heritage Not Hate clique. Charles and I encountered a number of white men and women sporting shirts that read PROUD MEMBER OF THE BASKET OF DEPLORABLES and hats saying MAKE AMERICA GREAT AGAIN. They puffed their chests like they'd just whipped a bull moose's ass in a fair fight. What was more startling — the number of Iron Eagle, SS, and swastika trin-kets being worn and offered for sale. I couldn't move when my eyes fell on a full-on Nazi officer's uniform on display and for sale. That was one thing. It was quite another to see how many white folks were clamoring to look at it up close.

I wondered, Has this been here all along? Is this the place where folks who hate me, and all other people who don't look and believe as they do, feel no shame about showing it? I think I knew the answer before I consciously asked myself that question, but it scared the hell out of me all the same. It still does. I dwelled on that moment when, a week later, news surfaced about a flyer being circulated around the University of Oklahoma campus. It was titled "Why White Women Shouldn't Date Black Men." It alleged that biracial children "probably won't be smart," black men "are much more likely to have STDs," and dating a black man "starts with rape and gets much worse."

I wondered how many of the thousands of people who visited Wanenmacher's that weekend believed those hateful things? How many of them might've tried to do harm to me or Lizzie, had they known we were engaged? This is terror.

Nearly all the people at the show seemed to be swapping, haggling, and hustling — all part and parcel of gun shows. Hell, when I was with Charles at another gun show, he saw a pink .22 rifle, the kind you might give to a Harley Quinn wannabe, and bought it because he just thought it was cute. He figured he might make it his truck rifle, the kind you keep on the gun rack in the back, just in case a doe crosses your path or you spot a coyote in the pasture. As Charles sauntered through the show, he had to fend off people asking *You selling? How much?* They just assumed he was selling because he was carrying the gun around with him. The scene reminded me of Jake and Elwood Blues, sitting in a posh restaurant and accosting a family at the table behind them: "Your women! I want to buy your women! The little girl, your daughters! Sell them to me! Sell me your children!"

At Wanenmacher's, I was both amused and horrified to see two old white men in a thoroughfare, gesticulating and arguing over an impromptu sell that seemed to be going awry.

"Why're you trying to Jew me down?"

"Why don't you just pay my asking price?"

"You're trying to give me a Mexican's price."

Every gun show enables haggling and hustling. You'll see folks with signs mounted on backpacks, strollers, oxygen tanks, and even the shirts on their backs, advertising a gun for whatever the asking price is. In this instance, the haggling apparently created a safe space for yet another sport: throwing around racial slurs.

At the Wanenmacher's gun show, folks ogled shotguns and rifles owned by dead presidents and generals. They haggled over the worth of various antique guns that no longer fired but held some value for someone who thought they were worth thousands. They bought their wives and girlfriends concealed-carry purses while purchasing for themselves calendars featuring half-naked (white) women holding exotic guns and one more banana clip for the assault rifle at home, because, well, you never know.

I began picking up gun magazines, to bring myself up to speed on gun culture, but mostly for the pictures: *Guns & Ammo, Concealed Carry Handguns, RECOIL, Gun Fighter,* and *Black Guns*. Was that *Black Guns* as opposed to *White Guns? Rainbow Guns? Polka Dot Guns?* On the cover it featured a tattooed white woman holding an EraThr3 Anorexia Rifle with Leupold LCD viewfinder. In the end I couldn't make it through a single article that day — gun-magazine prose read like an echo chamber. Readers didn't have to worry about reading anything "politically correct," and gun manufacturers didn't have to think for a minute that product placement wasn't the whole point.

We left the gun show and got back into Charles's truck. In the passenger's side, I sat with the Glock, still in its box, laid in my lap.

"Would you teach me how to shoot this thing?"

This was the next step. I was ready to become a responsible, licensed gun owner. I needed to know what it meant to have a gun in my house and to have the audacity to carry it in public.

"Yeah," Charles answered, with a jovial tone. "Sure. Teach you how next week."

THE DAY I got back home with my new gun, still in its box, I set it on my bed and looked at it for some time. I hadn't opened it at the gun show. I knew the gun inside the box had never been fired, and I knew it was mine. I didn't feel proud. What I felt was something more like fear. Like the fear I was taught to have for the God of the Old Testament, the being who was so merciful, He drowned the planet, cast out a favorite son, and told a father to murder his son to prove his love. Fear, the way I was taught to feel it as a black man trying to earn an education, navigate among the police, stay out of jail, and stay alive. I knew that the first time I lost respect for that pistol no larger than my fist, it could kill me — or get me killed.

I opened the box and picked up the Glock. I was amazed at how intuitive it was: the process of removing the empty magazine, putting it back, and racking the slide.

Was it really that easy?

A person with a gun tends to feel a lot like Superman with x-ray vision, laser sight, and Hulk-smash strength. Which is why telling that person not to *use* those super powers will generally result in the person looking at you like *you're* the lunatic.

I pointed the gun at the blank white bedroom wall in my second-story apartment and squeezed, feeling the hard click of the trigger, the soft tap of the hammer in an empty chamber. I put the gun back in its case, knowing that next week, the chamber would no longer be empty, and that this bit of polymer, plastic, and metal would no longer be an expensive paperweight, but a weapon so lethal, I wish we could un-invent it.

5

GRANDMOMME

AS I PREPARED for my odyssey into white gun culture, I knew that my having a gun would provoke white people's fear. I had already seen the look on Charles's face and those of some of Lizzie's friends when she introduced me as the man she was dating: one-half bemusement, one-half *How did this happen?*

I resented that look, and I resented that fear, and I knew they would only get worse once I had a gun. In this country, more than thirty Americans are murdered with guns every day. Fifteen of them are black. Black boys are ten times more likely than white boys to be thought of as older, and guilty; therefore they are more likely to be victims of police violence. Racial bias research shows that people believe "black men are more capable of causing harm in a hypothetical altercation and, troublingly, that police would be more justified in using force to subdue them, even if the men were unarmed." For a black man in possession of a gun, this data might raise some worries about white folks' misplaced fear. It gets even more problematic for a black man in the South.

A Tuskegee University study put a number on how many black folks have been hanged or burned for sins real and imagined without due process and without trial. In 1892 alone, 161 blacks were lynched. Between the years of 1890 and 1965, years when the dastardly Jim Crow laws were on the books in the South, 2,911 blacks were lynched in this country. That means an average of 39 blacks were lynched each year, every year, for seventy-five years. Now couple those soul-crushing stats with these. In 2011, the year Charles bought me my gun, the Centers for Disease Control and Prevention counted 460 people who had died by "legal intervention" involving the discharge of a firearm. That likely underreports the actual incidents. But we do know that black people were, between 1968 and 2011, from two to eight times more likely than whites to die at the hands of law officers. Which means that the number of police shootings of blacks in that year — and certainly today — is nearly equal to the average number of black people who were lynched in this country at the height of "separate but (un)equal."

The pure malice and hatred behind the Jim Crow–era lynchings compelled the black journalist Ida B. Wells to write a pamphlet in 1892 called "Southern Horrors." She chronicled many contemporary atrocities against blacks, and her report led her to a clear conclusion regarding black people and firearms: "The lesson this teaches and which every Afro-American should ponder well," Wells wrote, "is that a Winchester rifle should have a place of honor in every black home, and it should be used for that protection which the law refuses to give. When the white man who is always the aggressor knows, he runs as great a risk of biting the dust every time his Afro-American victim does, he will have greater respect for Afro-American life. The more the Afro-American yields and cringes and begs, the more he has to do so, the more he is insulted, outraged and lynched."

Into the twentieth century, white southerners continued to go to great lengths to prevent blacks from legally carrying firearms. Local ordinances and state laws gave local officials power to decide who had sufficient reason to carry one. In fact, amid the renewed racial tensions following World War II, Martin Luther King Jr., the same man who led the pacifist contingent of the civil rights movement, was denied a concealed-carry permit even after his house was bombed in 1956.

King was noted for his nonviolent — and ultimately winning — approach to civil rights reform. Nonetheless, a small militia devoted to the cause protected his house. King's friend and adviser Rev. Glenn Smiley called King's residence "an arsenal." But it was the likes of Malcolm X and the Black Panther Party that pushed the Second Amendment rights of blacks to the forefront of conversations about civil rights.

When the Oakland police stopped the Black Panthers' Huey Newton, Bobby Seale, and others in February 1967, a cop asked about the handguns and rifles in their possession.

"I don't have to give you anything but my identification, name, and address," Newton said.

"Who in the hell do you think you are?" one officer asked.

"Who in the hell do you think *you* are?" Newton stepped out of the vehicle, still holding his rifle.

"What are you going to do with that gun?" a cop asked.

"What are you going to do with *your* gun?" Newton replied.

A crowd surrounded them by now. Police tried to shoo the bystanders away. Newton insisted that California law allowed citizens to observe an arrest, so long as they did not interfere with it. He was yelling now. "If you try to shoot at me or if you try to take this gun," Newton said, "I'm going to shoot back at you, swine!"

Espoused by the Black Panthers and the NRA alike, the Second Amendment, as it is written, guarantees the right of every American to keep a gun in the home and on his or her person in public. The Panthers pushed this idea further, taking the view that the Second Amendment afforded them the right to take up arms against a fascist government. For the Panthers, racist police officers acted as an extension of a fascist government.

Six months after the incident with the Oakland police, there were thirty Panthers, four of them women. Each had a firearm of some kind — a .357 Magnum, a 12-gauge shotgun, or a .45-caliber pistol. Two years after the assassination of Malcolm X, the man who'd posed for an *Ebony* magazine cover in a black suit and tie as he held an M1 carbine, the

Panthers famously took to the steps of the California legislature, on May 2, 1967. They were protesting the Mulford Act of 1967, which repealed a law allowing open carry in the state of California. Bobby Seale read this statement:

> *The American people in general and the black people in particular must take careful note of the racist California legislature aimed at keeping the black people disarmed and powerless. Black people have begged, prayed, petitioned, demonstrated and everything else to get the racist power structure of America to right the wrongs which have historically been perpetuated against black people. The time has come for the black people to arm themselves against this terror before it is too late.*

This group of Black Panthers scared the 1960s version of the NRA so much, the organization voiced support for the Gun Control Act of 1968. Commenting in the NRA's in-house magazine, *American Rifleman,* the group's executive vice president, Franklin Orth, went out of his way to condemn mail-order sales of guns. After all, Lee Harvey Oswald had killed President John F. Kennedy with a gun he'd ordered through the US mail. "We do not think that any sane American," Orth said, "who calls himself an American, can object to placing into this bill the instrument which killed the president of the United States."

Now, we know the reasoning behind the law was not gun control, but rather *black* gun control. As the historian Da-

vid Babat writes, "The supposed aim of this bill was a reduc-
tion in crime, but an underlying motive was to keep black
militant groups from arming themselves with readily available and inexpensive weapons." And we now know that the
NRA's support of the Gun Control Act in fact led to a white
gun-buying bonanza. My grandmomme, Peggy Jean Connor, had deep experience in how a black person's gain in
personal dignity and freedom was received by white people.
They invariably viewed it as incitement.

THE PEGGY JEAN Connor I knew while growing up sat
through uncountable living-room screenings of *Forrest
Gump*. When the VHS tape committed technological sep-
puku rather than suffer abuse from me and my little sister,
Denise, any longer, Grandmomme consoled us while we
cried (she probably inwardly rejoiced). She lived in her own
home close to her daughter, my mother, and took Denise
and me on errands all over Hattiesburg. We were delight-
fully known as "Jean's grandbabies" then, as we are now.
At the end of each errand-running session, she rewarded
us with a treat of some sort — a toy we quickly lost interest in or a trip to the Hattiesburg Zoo. Grandmomme took
me to and from baseball practice when both of my parents
were at work; looked on as I learned karate with a ferocity I
later learned was genetic; kept the playbills from the plays
she watched me perform in; bought me a new suit for Eas-
ter every year until I was fifteen; spent way too much on
my roller skates; paid for my ear piercings; never called me

fat as a child, but rather "husky"; bought me all the books I showed even a casual interest in; took me to church on most Wednesdays and Sundays at Zion Chapel African Methodist Episcopal Church; and refused to let me believe I was anything other than exactly the grandson she'd always wanted.

I was just old enough to know that Velcro shoes meant I wouldn't have to tell myself the story about the goddamn bunny running around a tree when Grandmomme told me her story about Lawrence Guyot and Fannie Lou Hamer.

Understand, now, that Guyot is a major figure in the civil rights movement in Mississippi. One of the defining moments of his life was his trip to Winona, Mississippi, to bail out Fannie Lou Hamer and two others who had been arrested for standing in a bus-stop area reserved for white people. (Hamer, a contemporary of Grandmomme and Guyot, had also endured an involuntary hysterectomy at the hands of a white doctor while having surgery to remove a tumor. Why? The state of Mississippi — a bona fide mother-*fucker* — wanted to reduce its number of poor black people.)

Once Guyot made his intentions known in Winona, local police forced him to strip naked. Then nine of them beat him bloody for four hours, even threatening to set his penis and testicles aflame. This is the kind of story I heard as a child. Grandmomme's stories. I was sitting on her porch steps while she talked and watered plants, which did nothing but annoy me when I'd lose a baseball in their thickets. "Lawrence lived through it," Grandmomme said. "Me too." She spritzed an azalea with a spray bottle, and paused.

"We didn't always feel like we would live to see the next morning."

Just as she was about to bend over and spray some more, I asked, "What else? About Mr. Guyot? Y'all were friends?"

Grandmomme smiled, put down the spray bottle, and took a seat next to me. "Let me tell you about Lawrence — and a bit about your Grandmomme — back when your daddy was still squeezing you into a napkin."

"How could I be squeezed into a —"

"Hush," she said.

GUYOT SERVED AS chairman and director of the Mississippi Freedom Democratic Party in 1964. Grandmomme, Peggy Jean Connor, was its executive secretary. One year before he died, in November 2012, Guyot recorded an oral history, and he mentioned Grandmomme in it.

One story in particular gets to the heart of Grandmomme as seen through the eyes of her peers and historians — how the world views her and how she viewed the world. Grandmomme and other delegates chosen from the Mississippi Freedom Democratic Party crashed the 1964 Democratic National Convention in Atlantic City. They challenged the all-white delegation for excluding blacks from the political process. She was alongside Fannie Lou Hamer when Hamer gave her famous "I question America" speech about voter suppression and law enforcement's racist violence. This remains one of the crucibles of Grandmomme's life. But Guyot's oral history adds a dramatic coda.

"Peggy Jean Connor was the little, sweet, nice lady who," Guyot said, "when the bus was coming back from Atlantic City, some whites [was] trying to stop it. So she got up to the bus driver and took a long knife. She said, Now, if this bus stops, your head comes off." Story is, the bus driver kept driving.

It wasn't until I was in grade school that I began to understand, in the smallest sense, Grandmomme's stature according to historians, journalists, politicians, and fellow civil rights activists like Guyot.

GRANDMOMME WAS BORN on October 29, 1932, in Hattiesburg, Mississippi. She began working in her aunt Hattie's beauty parlor as a shampoo girl when she was eleven years old and graduated from Garrett's Beauty School in 1946. At fourteen, she became a licensed beautician. The state's minimum age requirement for work was sixteen. She lied on the application. Grandmomme graduated from Eureka High School at eighteen and did a year of college work at Royal Street Extension in Hattiesburg. Two years later, she met Dennie Frank Connor, an army man, and on April 14, 1952, she married him. Their marriage is recorded in the colored-marriage-license record book in the same Forrest County Courthouse Grandmomme would later picket so my mother could attend the same school as a white child.

When Grandmomme's aunt Hattie decided to leave for New Jersey, she left her salon to Grandmomme, who became responsible for paying the store rent and paying employees. Her father, John Henry, built a sign for her. It read JEAN'S BEAUTY SHOP and was erected above the salon at 510 Mobile Street — just four blocks from where she lived then and until recently. She had barely reached legal drinking age when she became one of just a handful of female sole proprietors in Hattiesburg. In those years, she paid her poll tax, a registration fee the state charged all those who wanted to vote. First instituted in Georgia in 1871, the poll tax was one in a series of insidious ventures through which the segregated South disenfranchised black voters during the broken promise of Reconstruction. While the tax was small — in many cases it was just one or two dollars — any amount was large for the mostly poor rural population of blacks. In 1937, *Breedlove v. Suttles* challenged the legality of the poll tax, but not until *Harman v. Forssenius* in 1965 would the court strike down the racist poll-tax laws, under the Fourteenth Amendment of the Constitution.

As a young woman in the 1950s, Grandmomme volunteered to bring money for the poll tax, hers and others', to the courthouse. Many blacks in Hattiesburg feared the circuit court clerk and registrar — a big white man named Theron Lynd who was so racist, he'd likely bring extra tiki torches to a parade. Lynd, and Lynd alone, had the power to say who could and could not vote in Forrest County, Mississippi. Folks dropped off their money at Grandmomme's shop, and then she faithfully walked to the courthouse, paid for those who were too afraid to pay for themselves, and collected their receipts. "He treated me like the dirtiest mangiest dog you ever saw," Grandmomme said. And every time she went, she took the venom Lynd spat at her, and walked out proudly.

WHILE MY GLOCK was still new, I called Grandmomme to ask whether Guyot's story was really true. Had she been willing to cut off a man's head with a knife? "This is what Mr. Guyot said, Grandmomme," I said.

"Lawrence," she said.

"Huh?"

"He might be dead, but he'd prefer to be called Lawrence."

"Yes, ma'am." I waited, thinking she might have more to say on the subject.

I waited some more. "Grandmomme?"

"I'm thinking." Her tone of voice lay somewhere between annoyed and downright *pissed*.

"Never happened," Grandmomme said eventually.

"Huh?"

"His story about me. It never happened."

"Wait — *really?*" I asked.

"I've heard it before," she said. "Folks just want to believe it's true — mythologizing. Nobody ever bothered to check with me, though. I tell you this. I've never got anything done with guns and knives. But just because I was nonviolent doesn't mean I wasn't angry. Just like you, Sugar."

6

THERE IS NO TRY

A WEEK OR so after Charles had escorted me to the gun show, I was at his house again, after carrying my unloaded firearm in the back of my truck. From my apartment in Norman, I'd traveled more than a hundred miles.

The feeling of traveling with a firearm, even an unloaded one in a plastic carrying case, didn't sit well with me. Not because I was afraid of an unloaded gun, but because I feared what might happen if an Oklahoma highway patrolman pulled me over and spotted it on the bench seat in the back. From that day on, when I traveled with my gun, I kept it unloaded, in its box, beneath the driver's seat, where prying eyes were not likely to see it when looking in through the window.

There are no felonies on my record. I am, in the eyes of my government, an upstanding citizen. Yet I felt it necessary to take the same precautions as a wanted criminal because my skin is brown and my hair is curly. And yes, I realize that those who believe black men have something to hide could take this quite literally as an example of a black man doing just that.

JIMMY HADN'T BLINKED when I'd asked him earlier that week to go with me to Frank's Gun & Repair to get the ammunition I'd need. He even drove. I'd already asked Charles to take me.

"Ask Jimmy," he said. "Jimmy knows Frank too."

Maybe Jimmy sensed my apprehension about walking into a gun store alone. Even beside him, I didn't feel the least bit capable of asking Frank for what I needed. I felt closed in and frozen. But Jimmy began to chat up Frank, and Frank showed his affinity for Jimmy, and by extension Charles, and he had no problem retrieving the nine-millimeter shells for my gun and the .22-caliber shells for the pistol Lizzie would be using. She'd shoot with us because it was a chance for her to be with her men. Jimmy paid for the shells, another act of kindness. Frank put them in a plastic bag and presented the straps to Jimmy.

"Y'all go shoot 'em up now."

It's not every day that I'm expressly told to *go shoot* anything, and I couldn't think of a time when it had been said to me with a smile.

AT THE HOUSE, Charles showed me how to load the magazine for my Glock 26. The magazine is miniature for this model, by Glock standards, with just room enough for seven rounds, but that is also the same number of rounds provided by the full-size Colt 1911. The small magazine is part of the genius of the "Baby Glock." The gun can be holstered almost anywhere on your person without bulge or discomfort. Some folks even carry it in the front pocket of their pants. The former NFL star Plaxico Burress rather famously carried his gun, sans holster, at a New York City night club in 2008 and managed not only to shoot himself in the leg, but also got sentenced to time for criminal possession of a firearm. He spent nearly two years behind bars. Plus, *he shot himself in the leg*. So I don't need to try front-of-the-pants.

I was surprised at how tough it was to load my gun's magazine. As I popped each additional bullet into the magazine, the spring beneath it became harder to depress. After I'd loaded five rounds, I was having a hard time loading the sixth. Charles had to do it for me. But not without chiding me to "use those muscles of yours." I saw this man, whose hands ached sometimes with arthritis, load the last two bullets without incident. The way Charles inserted those shells into the magazine had little to do with hand strength and everything to do with technique. His thumb and index finger were set against the magazine. His thumb pressed on top of the round, so the bullet wouldn't slip. He depressed the bullet and slid it back into the magazine. He made it look easy.

I noticed he didn't immediately snap the magazine into the pistol, not at his kitchen table. He simply laid it into the box beside the pistol and closed the box. A pistol can do you no harm, even if the magazine is loaded, if the magazine is not inside the pistol. I would later learn how many people insert a full magazine into a pistol just because they'd gone through the trouble of filling the magazine with bullets, and then leave it that way. Charles never did this, and I knew he'd lived his entire life around guns with nary a bad incident. To say I watched him is to say I mimicked him in every way I could.

My trying so hard is likely what set me up to have my feelings hurt once Charles, Jimmy, Lizzie, and I got to target practice. We were about one hundred yards from the house, in front of a tree line. Livestock was cordoned from the site. We used Charles's truck as a staging area. This is where targets, bullets, gun boxes, earmuffs, and guns were put when not in use.

I was to learn later that some folks wear a hat for protection from spent casings, which can burn your neck. Most folks wear eye protection for the same reason, unless, like me, you walk around four-eyed all the time. And everybody needs to wear ear protection because the sound of a gun firing repeatedly can have the same effect on your hearing as Nickelback blared at the volume of an air-raid siren. Your eardrums tend to want to bleed out and die.

Jimmy handed out the ear protection, and Charles let me step up first. In truth, I didn't want to go first. I really would rather have watched someone else. But Charles loved to put people on the spot to see how they react to pressure or to find out whether they were as skilled as they claimed to be. I'd first learned this when Charles found out that I worked as a mechanic. Minutes into one visit, he took me to one of the trucks he was having a problem with, which was most of them, and asked me what I thought. I gave him my two cents on the matter, and he casually mentioned that the mechanic he'd asked to look at the truck had said the same.

On this day, I took a few steps forward to the spot he'd pointed to and tried to think about what it might take to hit the target Jimmy had mounted in front of the tree line. I waited an instant. Then I asked Charles what I should do.

"Line up the sights with the target," he said, "and pull the trigger." I figured I would have to settle for that. Then he spoke again. "Now don't hold it like this."

Holding it like this was demonstrated as holding the gun sideways — my wrist had turned ninety degrees counter-clockwise.

Like I bang.

Like a criminal.

I did my best to shrug off Charles's criticism, even laughed it off. I tried to put the gun sights on the target's bull's-eye. When I fired, I missed. I missed terribly. And I continued to miss terribly with the next six rounds. When my Glock locked up, with the slide no longer in the ready-to-fire position, I knew it was spent. But I wasn't done. I walked back to the truck, took the magazine out of the gun, and went about the business of trying to reload it. I managed to load only five shells. The sixth seemed impossible to maneuver, and I was perfectly frustrated. So I slid the magazine back into the gun and waited my turn. When I was up again, I tried to will the gun on target, which is all I could think to do. I held the gun tight. I closed one eye, and tried to stop my hands from shaking. Then I squeezed the trigger. But nothing happened.

I held the gun straight out in front of me because I didn't want to point it at Charles, and I turned around to look back at him. He'd seen it happen, or, more precisely, had seen nothing happen. He walked over to me and calmly took the gun from my hand, then stepped between me and the target, so I was out of harm's way. He looked the gun over for just a few seconds. Then he smashed his palm into the magazine, snapping it into place, pulled back on the slide, ejecting a round, and then fired the gun three times. He handed it back to me, with the barrel facing away from us, and told me to shoot. I fired the last two rounds, hitting nothing but the white of the paper, nowhere near the bull's-eye.

"Those Glocks, they don't like cheap ammunition," he said.

I had dreaded this excursion precisely because I didn't want to embarrass myself, or worse, hurt myself. That sense of caution just makes me an adult. But I didn't expect the embarrassment to cut so hard. I didn't expect to feel physically inadequate when loading a gun, firing a gun, and then not just missing the target, but *woefully* missing it.

I was pouty and angry for the rest of the day. Lizzie knew enough to leave me alone with that. But that was also the day I decided it was not enough to be proficient with a fire-arm. I needed to be *better* with one than the vast majority of gun enthusiasts who might see my inadequacy and turn the knife with a quip about how I held my gun sideways. Yes, I needed to become a better shot than Charles.

Also, I was certainly interested to find out if the self-appointed guardians of the Second Amendment would learn to tolerate my quest. I was a good guy. And now I had a gun. Would I be seen as a good guy with a gun?

But first I needed to get to be an expert with one. And I wouldn't enlist Charles's help. I was on a mission to become a Jedi Master with a gun, and I needed to do this my way, and there would be no more trying. As Master Yoda said, "Do. Or do not. There is no try."

WHEN I ARRIVED home that day, I found myself replaying the scene in *Good Will Hunting* when Matt Damon, as the working-class Southie savant Will Hunting, trash-talks a Harvard boy at a bar: "You dropped a hundred and fifty grand on fuckin' education you could've got for a buck fifty in late charges at the public library." You can also get an education in target shooting, defensive shooting, cleaning guns, the history of guns, and the disassembly and reassembly of guns for free on YouTube. That's where I chose to start the hands-on portion of my gun education.

I first wanted to find the proper way to clean and maintain my gun. So I went to Academy Sports and found a handgun-cleaning kit I thought would do the job. Then I searched YouTube for cleaning tutorials. I found a middle-aged white dude who went by the alias hickok45 who was using a Glock 27 to demonstrate his cleaning technique. The first thing he did, the first thing that even I knew already we should all do, was demonstrate that the magazine was empty. Then he racked the slide back multiple times to show there were no rounds in the chamber. Finally, he pulled the trigger, dry-firing the weapon to further illustrate the point that this gun was safe and a danger only if you threw it. It was, essentially, a $500 paperweight.

He told viewers that the trigger needed to be depressed "before you break it down." I noticed how he wrapped his right hand around the back of the pistol, pulled back slightly on the slide, and depressed a couple of small levers on each side of the slide to release it. The slide houses the firing pin, or striker, and the extractor on a semiautomatic pistol. It took me several minutes to figure out the correct combination of finesse and strength needed to get my slide off. Once I did, I felt a sense of accomplishment. I'd essentially just made my gun two halves of a whole.

I continued to follow along. I removed the spring and then the barrel from the slide. I learned that this was as far as I would ever need to go: just four parts — the magazine, the slide, the spring, and the barrel — need to be removed from a Glock to begin cleaning it. This, I later learned, is called a field strip. It's so easily done that, once you get the hang of it, it becomes a sort of parlor trick. I eventually found another video of a man field-stripping his Glock .380

in nine seconds. Now I watched as hickok45 sprayed lubricant inside and outside his gun barrel. Then I listened to him talk about how picking a lubricant was a lot like picking motor oil: everybody has a favorite.

While hickok45 let the lubricant soak, he picked up a toothbrush and began to lightly brush it across the top of the receiver, the body of the pistol leading toward the pistol grip. He was adamant about keeping oil or lubricant off the brush and the receiver itself. "I keep it far away from that." I used the toothbrush-like brush that came with my kit and flicked it across my Glock, which hadn't been fired twenty times yet, while hickok45 talked about getting the corrosion off the receiver. I learned that corrosion and bits of lead, copper, or carbon can damage a gun — they can make it jam or render it inoperable. I watched him dip a Q-tip, something I did not have on hand, into a small cap of alcohol and lightly dab it into the crevices of the receiver that a toothbrush couldn't reach — not unlike flossing your teeth.

When he was done with that, he picked up the slide and ran his toothbrush up and down its inside. I followed along, running my toothbrush up and down my slide, picking up only the lightest buildup of brown tarnish. Hickok45 repeated his use of the Q-tip inside the slide. Then he ran the toothbrush over the spring before moving back to the barrel.

This is when he reached for what is called his cleaning rod and a small piece of cloth. I had both in my cleaning kit. Following hickok45, I fixed the cloth to my cleaning rod and shoved it straight down the barrel, in the same direction that a bullet would fire. I pulled it out and ran it through three more times, with three more cloth patches. Hickok45 touched a tiny amount on the rails of the receiver, and on the tip of the slide, and then reassembled his Glock.

In fewer than fifteen minutes, he'd shown me the routine. It was so simple, I performed the task four more times —from disassembly to cleaning to reassembly—before I thought I might know just enough to be dangerous. Then I made a point of cleaning the gun three times a day for the next week, so it became a comfortable habit. A week before I'd first cleaned my gun, I was so afraid of it, all I could do was stare at it. Now it didn't seem like the kind of lethal device that might leap from its box to dig straight into my jugular. It was more like a tool, and I was just beginning to learn to care for it. A tool I could even imagine starting to master.

7

WALDO

IN OKLAHOMA, YOU must earn a handgun license to conceal-carry or openly carry your firearm. If I can see your gun on your person in the street and you have a license, you are operating within the law in Oklahoma. The same is true if your gun is concealed. However, you do not need a license of any kind to openly carry a firearm on your property.

The number of gun owners with a concealed-carry license has nearly tripled nationwide, from 4.6 million licenses in 2007, the year before Barack Obama was elected president, to 12.9 million in 2015. That's an increase of a million new concealed-carry licenses a year. In 2014 alone, 1.7 million Americans received concealed-carry licenses. My own state, Oklahoma, counts 217,724 permits as of March 2015. Overall, 5.2 percent of the US population is licensed to carry a concealed firearm, with five states counting at least 10 percent of their respective populations as concealed-carry gun owners.

Since Oklahoma performs a background check on any-one who applies for a handgun license, charges money for processing the background check, and makes you reapply every ten years (at a maximum), you've got to really want to be right with the law to apply. I don't like the idea of ex-plaining how the law works to a police officer who might stop me. I'd rather have my handgun license on me, and show it right there. I'm a black man. I don't leave the house without my walking papers.

So I took the eight-hour course, with a guy I privately dubbed Waldo, or Self-Reliant Man, since he seemed like the kind of guy who had read Emerson's "Self-Reliance" enough to quote it. I passed my written exam. The Cleve-land County Sheriff's Department fingerprinted me. I sent my paperwork to the Oklahoma Bureau of Investigation, and it sent me back an I.D. With that bit of plastic, I could inform anybody who needed to know that I was legally li-censed to carry a loaded concealed firearm everywhere that device for ending life was permitted. But I wasn't ready to exercise that right because, frankly, I still couldn't hit a bull's-eye at ten yards. To learn more about this skill, I again consulted YouTube.

I watched videos about things like sight alignment, sight picture, pumpkins on posts, and aligning the three rectan-gular men. I watched videos about proper stance, breathing techniques, and the best way to grip a gun. I watched vid-eos about letting the bang of the gun surprise you and how important it is to think about squeezing rather than pulling a trigger; how a squeeze is more akin to a pleasant hug and a pull more of a yank. I watched videos about ammunition, learning how the weight of a full or half-full magazine can balance or imbalance a weapon. I learned how to figure out which of my eyes was the dominant one and the importance of creating an isosceles triangle with my arms with each shot. I read and read again *The Gun Digest's Book of the Glock* to try to internalize the workings of my pocket Glock 26.

I started traveling twice a week to the indoor pistol range in my town, Norman, Oklahoma, where I'd taken my concealed-carry course. I'd take my unloaded pistol from beneath my bed, still in its case, a box of Winchester nine-millimeter ammunition I kept in a locked box in the closet, and store both items beneath the driver's seat of my truck. I walked into the building, which was a long rectangle, with a small foyer and a meeting room adjacent to the range itself. In the foyer, I paid the ten-dollar range fee and bought a target for a dollar. I opened a door to my left, stepped onto the range, and procured a stall. I unloaded the pistol box, ammunition box, and earmuffs that I always left in the truck, and went about the business of loading and firing.

But after two solid months of nearly no progress, I became frustrated. I was enduring the occasional quizzical look and snide comment from other patrons too. The ones that stuck bit through to the marrow of who I am. *Ain't you supposed to be shooting a basketball?* and *Hold it sideways, it's more your people's style* were two of the less clever barbs along those lines. But the one that pissed me off most was more direct.

"You any good with that pistol?"

This came from an elderly white man passing by my stall. He hadn't seen me shoot. He was hanging on to what little hair remained around his ears and wore a work shirt, blue jeans, and beat-to-shit black orthopedic shoes. He carried a bag the size of a small backpack over his shoulder. It looked just big enough to hold something small enough to kill a room full of people in mere seconds.

Searching his face, I found that he was sincere, so I answered his question.

"Not really, no."

I tried to smile about it, to smile *through it,* as he walked down the corridor to an open shooting bay. Still in stride, he called back over his shoulder.

"Well, keep at it. You can't get any worse."

I knew he meant encouragement, but I felt angry that I'd become someone to fucking *console* at the gun range. I couldn't have that. I needed to become so diabolically methodical about what I was doing, so fiercely fantastic, that I could inspire in others the fear that they inspired in me, simply by murdering paper targets. I learned several things about myself that day. I wasn't nearly as scared of being a victim of gun violence as I was of this utterly visceral need to radiate machismo. I learned — machismo aside — that I needed to keep digging. I needed to find better and more purposeful ways of shooting, rather than shooting for shoot-ing's sake.

I needed a teacher.

Someone who was willing to suffer me enough to teach me what I needed to know about marksmanship, defen-sive shooting, and gun safety. Because my life is a romping Greek tragicomedy, I had no choice but to chortle ruefully when I learned that the best person in the Cleveland County area to teach me what I needed to know was the guy I had privately dubbed Waldo, who'd taught my concealed-carry course. I dreaded asking him for help.

At the counter at the range, I asked if Waldo was avail-able. The fella behind the counter smirked and called out over his shoulder.

"Guy out here wants a private."

Waldo emerged from an office door behind the counter and looked me up and down. "When do you want to start?"

I couldn't help smiling. We set a date and time — Mon-day the following week. Thus began my formal education on skillful use of the thing that could have put an end to Me-dusa, Cerberus, and Typhon and still have two in the maga-zine for Charybdis and Scylla — each.

WHEN WALDO MET me in the lobby of the range, he snatched a paper target and then escorted me out to the range proper while asking me about my history of shooting. I explained that I'd been coming to the range pretty steadily but had had no formal training. He asked whether any living, breathing person not on the Internet had given me any instruction whatsoever. I told him that the extent of my education outside YouTube had come from a father-in-law whose most direct verbal instruction had been *Don't hold it like this.* Waldo nodded. I felt he understood where I was coming from. He hung the paper target on a pulley rope and then he set about looking my gun over.

I saw how careful and pensive he was as he looked inside the empty magazine well of the gun and then slid the slide back three times before locking it in place and peering down the slide as if searching for an answer to a question that had plagued him for weeks. Satisfied, he put the gun back in the case and inspected the magazine I'd loaded with five rounds. Then, one by one, he took the rounds out and put them beside the gun in the case. Next he was on to the ammunition I'd brought. He glanced at the box, reading it, and then pulled out a round and gave it to me.

"Let me see you load it."

I took it from him, knowing I was probably going to embarrass myself. I managed to get the single bullet into the magazine without much incident. He paused and nodded.

"OK, I can see why you have a problem loading."

He'd seen me load only one round, and I hadn't told him a single thing about how I was having the toughest time forcing bullets into a magazine less than half the size of a full-size Glock's. Though I'd tried to remember how I'd seen Charles do it and had watched *hours* of right-wing white guys on YouTube who could just punch the little jacketed bastards in there, I still had trouble.

"Your fingers are strong enough," he said. "You're just not using your whole thumb."

Waldo showed me how to properly position my fingers to gain a greater grip on the slippery metal bullet and place it in the magazine in such a manner that it couldn't first slip away. I followed suit and was astounded at how much easier it was to put the bullet in the magazine. In only a couple of minutes, I'd filled a gun's magazine for the first time in my life. In that same lesson, Waldo showed me how to set my feet so that I was never off balance when the gun fired. He demonstrated not only how to align my sights properly but how to correct misalignments. He'd diagnose why I'd missed where I'd expected to hit. He taught me how to use the pad, the pinch portion, of my index finger to squeeze the trigger. He showed me how to inhale and exhale with the trigger squeeze.

In that first lesson, I didn't shoot a target that was more than three yards away. Waldo placed an emphasis on working through the fundamentals rather than striking the X in the middle of the target every time. I never shot more than three rounds without taking a rest. I learned I was making myself tired by shooting several rounds in one session, and as a result, I got lazy about form. Resting just five minutes allowed my body and mind to recover from the intense focus and strain I put on it with each squeeze of the trigger.

Before the lesson was over, Waldo picked a brass casing

off the floor and had me pack up and follow him into an empty room. Once there, he sent me home with a drill I've come to believe has done the most to make me a marksman. It had to do with trigger control and focus. Waldo had me step behind him as he, once again, checked my empty gun. He reset the action and then pointed the gun straight out in front of him, with his right hand, at a blank white wall. With his left hand, he balanced the brass casing on top of the front sight, so that it stood atop the end of the barrel of the gun. This itself is a feat. But then he methodically squeezed the trigger. When I heard the hammer strike the gun, the brass casing still hadn't moved.

The point of the exercise is to maintain an easy but sustained trigger pull without jerking the weapon. To remain steady, calm, and aligned, so that the firing of the gun comes as a surprise. Most new shooters have a problem with anticipating the recoil of their handgun, even when trying their damnedest not to do exactly that. When Waldo had me perform the drill — mounting the brass for me after I couldn't do it myself, in my first four tries — the brass fell off as I pulled the trigger, as if a stiff breeze had knocked it over. This was also a lesson in being a craftsperson who doesn't blame the tools.

"When you can do that several times without the brass coming off," Waldo said, "you're a shooter."

So this became part of my routine, part of my new obsession. I spent fifteen minutes twice a day for two weeks just trying to mount the brass on the narrow front sight before I could do it without incident. And I spent a full month watching the brass fall off as soon as I felt the pressure release the firing pin in my Glock. Eventually, I could with some regularity pull the trigger without upsetting the brass, but not enough to do it more than twice in a row. Still, the better I got with that drill, the better I got at killing paper targets. I could see my groupings getting smaller. I learned how to focus the sight on the front barrel before slightly blurring the sights on the rear of the barrel to get a true and accurate picture of where I was aiming.

I could see my mistakes as soon as I made them, and I could correct them. I was beginning to feel in control of this firearm. I was beginning to believe it was an extension of not just my arm, but my will.

I learned the difference between marksmanship, which has everything to do with focus, precision, and consistency, and defensive shooting, which is purely about primed responses to the danger at hand. I did not just want to be a good marksman. I wanted the knowledge of self-defense so many other Americans claim they want, claim as the reason for walking around with a gun. They know how to use one, or so they would have the rest of us believe. I wanted to know what they know or, at least, think they know. In a self-defense situation, I learned, I was not going to have time to draw, align my front and rear sights, control my breathing, and then fire when ready. Many confrontations take place with only an arm's length between attacker and victim. With just a moment to act, I'd already have to know how to draw from a concealed-carry holster, sight down the barrel, and rapidly pull, rather than squeeze, the trigger, aiming at my attacker with the goal of leaving the fight alive. Making an effort to kill was not as important as getting to safety and protecting any loved ones present.

The better a marksman I became, and the faster at drawing from the holster, the more I came to believe that too much could go wrong in such a situation. What would happen if I didn't get my shot off first? Or if my attacker stopped my hand as I made a move toward the gun at the front of my pants by raising my shirt with my left hand? What if the gun was knocked from my hand or ended up in the hands of my attacker? Worst, what if I *killed* that person? I couldn't believe killing another person under any circumstances could be a small thing. I don't know that I could bring myself to do that — no matter the danger.

The defensive-shooting part of my education was the most difficult and, ultimately, the most instructive. I learned what it takes to be prepared to take a life in self-defense, and that I wanted no part of it. I was my Grandmomme's grandson.

8

WHITE NRA

THE NATIONAL RIFLE Association's NRA Family website has published an article about Davy Crockett. In it, we learn what a crack shot Crockett was, using a rifle he nicknamed Old Betsy. He was so good that when, as an unknown from back east, he hit the center of the bull's-eye from one hundred yards at a shooting contest in Little Rock, Arkansas, folks called it a chance shot. There was no way the boy from back east could be *that* good from *that* distance.

But this was Davy Fuckin' Crockett, soon to be known as King of the Wild Frontier and shit. He took offense. So he shot again. This time, though, no hole could be seen in that target. Folks in attendance clearly thought the man's true skill could be called having none at all. He'd simply been lucky the first time. But Crockett walked up to the target and searched it with his finger, whereupon he found what he was looking for. Satisfied, he turned toward the dubious crowd. "Tell you what. If you don't find two bullets, you can use me as the target the next round."

This story became one of many that launched the man into folklore. He was in his twenties when he joined up with Andrew Jackson — then a slave-owning planter and colonel of the Tennessee militia — to fight the Creek Indians, who'd had the audacity to fight back at Fort Mims in Alabama just to the south of Crockett's home state of Tennessee. Through his Tennessee guile and charm, and his own good looks, I suppose, he followed Andrew Jackson's bloody footprints to rise to the rank of colonel in Tennessee's militia. After two terms as a US congressman, Crockett still had a thirst for war. He saw fit to head to Texas to defend four walls in San Antonio, along with fewer than two hundred other poor bastards, against five thousand professional soldiers in the army of the Mexican general López de Santa Anna. Today we remember those Texan men for picking off sixteen hundred out of five thousand soldiers and losing a battle that lasted twelve days.

And boy! Could Davy Crocket ever hunt bear! "Armed with his Bowie knife and his trusty musket, 'Old Betsy,'" according to the NRA website, "he would head out with his sons, a friend, or just himself in search of his favorite prey. Stories of Davy's bear-hunting adventures spread far and wide — in his books as well as in books written about him." Huzzah for the man who takes pleasure in shooting animals who can't shoot back!

It was in his books that Crockett revealed the man he

truly was, which is not the man as depicted by the NRA. At a time when many whites were looking for a way to rise above or remain above folks with a brown complexion — be they American Indian, black, or Mexican — Crockett became the first public redneck of note. The historian Laura Browder notes that Crockett's false autobiographical accounts "included stories in which Crockett boasted of boiling an Indian to make medicine for his pet bear's stomachache, bragged that he could 'swallow a nigger whole without choking if you butter his head and pin his ears back,' and described Mexicans and Cubans as 'degenerate outlaws,' "Indians as 'red niggers,' and African Americans as 'ape-like caricatures of humanity.'"

When the nation was on the brink of civil war and racism was the currency of the day, Crockett chose to plunge into its depths. He cloaked himself in the muck of the cesspool and continued the tradition of whites making themselves feel better at the expense of people who look or think or worship differently.

Crockett would later try to distance himself from these racist statements in his authorized autobiography, *A Narrative Life of David Crockett of the State of Tennessee,* published in 1834. In that volume, Crockett explains away his earlier writings, such as his pseudo-memoir *Sketches and Eccentricities,* as full of "catchpenny errors." He claimed that others placed "in my mouth such language as would disgrace even an outlandish African," either knowingly or unknowingly re-showcasing his primitive xenophobia. By this time, it had become inconvenient for him to take a stance as an avowed racist. Three decades later slavery was abolished. Crockett's rhetoric is hateful and malicious, a historical forerunner of the brand of speech that President Donald Trump used for the same reasons to assume the highest office in the nation. It's also the kind of rhetoric that has made the NRA a juggernaut lobbyist for "gun rights" in this country, a fear-mongering force that will never represent my concerns as a black man.

MAY 21, 1977, was the day the National Rifle Association changed, the day it revolted against its earlier goals and principles and mutated into the institution we know today. Accounts of this transformation can make it sound like a legend, a mythic event, but it was indeed a political coup carried out with zeal by white men who were concerned that the NRA had become "soft." On that day in Cincinnati, Ohio, a long-developed plan to change the direction of the NRA was put into action over several hours and well into the night. The way guns were thought about, advertised, promoted, litigated, and perceived in America was about to change.

By the time the old-guard members of the NRA's board figured out that a portion of the membership previously believed to be a fringe group was about to oust them, it was too late. The hostile takeover included the election of a fella named Harlon Carter as the organization's new executive vice president. Two years earlier, Carter had founded the

NRA's lobbying arm, the Institute for Legislative Action. It was responsible for first publicizing what would become the consistent forty-year stance of the NRA concerning legislation meant to curtail our country's rampant gun violence: "We can win it on a simple concept— *No compromise. No gun legislation.*" This from a man who at age seventeen had admitted to shooting and killing a younger teenage boy in a questionable situation he described as self-defense. Also during the year of Carter's ascendency, 1977, the NRA formed its now infamous super PAC, which funnels money to favored lawmakers. It is the most powerful special-interest group in the nation.

The NRA had been founded by a journalist and Civil War veteran to teach marksmanship as a skill for sportsmen and hunters. In 1939, the NRA president, Karl Frederick, couldn't conceive of a reason why a person should openly carry a gun. "I have never believed in the general practice of carrying weapons," Frederick testified before Congress. "I think it should be sharply restricted and only under licenses." Frederick even believed the right to a gun for the means of self-defense is "not to be found in the Constitution." This statement is even more interesting if you know that Frederick won the gold medal in individual and team pistol events at the 1920 Summer Olympic Games and captained the US Olympic shooting team in 1948.

But by 1977 the NRA was under siege for what the rebels perceived as its lack of interest in and downright inability to battle forthcoming gun legislation at a time of great violence in the United States. One of the last straws for the insurgents was the NRA board's plan to move the organization's premises away from Washington, D.C., to the middle of the country — Colorado Springs. The old guard hoped to build a $30 million recreational facility, called the National Outdoor Center, in New Mexico, to continue the NRA's mission of teaching sportsmen. They set this goal despite a dramatic drop in interest, as evidenced by a decrease in the number of hunting licenses issued: from 40 million in 1970 to just 14 million.

With the 1977 "Cincinnati Revolution," the old-school NRA was history. The hardline mutineers soon cracked down on members of Congress all over the country. Even the Republican senator from Kansas, Bob Dole, felt the tight grip of the NRA during his 1980 presidential run. "You have to have a litmus test every five minutes or you're considered wavering," he said.

This kind of squeezing helped the NRA successfully push through the Firearm Owners' Protection Act of 1986, which made it legal to sell rifles and handguns across state lines while making it impossible for the federal government to institute a nationwide database for guns and gun owners — a feature of other technologically and economically advanced countries. Legislators who didn't like the Firearm Owners' Protection Act voted for it anyway, fearing what the NRA might do to them if they didn't. When the Brady Handgun Violence Protection Act — which mandated a five-day waiting period for any person looking to purchase a firearm and

mandated a federal background check — was near to becoming law in 1991 (it was not finally enacted until 1994),
the vice president of the NRA, Robert Corbin, invoked the
Alamo during a speech at the association's annual meeting
in San Antonio, speaking to more than ten thousand members: "What if there had been a Brady Bill 150 years ago?" he
said. "What if they had to wait seven days to get their rifles
to come to the Alamo and fight?"

"This bill is treachery," the NRA member Elodie McKee
told the *Washington Post* at the same meeting. "It's the ugly
foot in the door. If President Bush doesn't veto this bill, he
will betray women, and women won't let him forget it."

This passionate rhetoric marked the birth of the NRA as
we know it today. An NRA with a fifteen-person shooting
range in the basement of its headquarters in Fairfax, Virginia. An NRA that can boast a membership that has included not only eight former presidents but celebrities such
as Tom Selleck, Karl Malone, and one-time association
president Charlton Heston. An NRA that declared more
than $227 million on its 2010 IRS Form 990, with $100
million coming from membership fees alone. This is how
the NRA can afford to pay ten of its top executives more
than $250,000 annually, with its executive director of gen-
eral operations, Kayne B. Robinson, making just over $1
million. With nearly five million members, today's NRA exists almost exclusively to raise hell and fight against legislation of any kind that could institute any measure of gun
control. Executive Vice President Wayne LaPierre has said

as much over and over again. Here's how he put it at the
NRA's annual meeting in 2002:

> We must declare that there are no shades of gray in
> American freedom. It's black and white, all or noth-
> ing, you're with us or against us. There are not flavors
> of freedom. You can't like yours, but not mine. There
> are not classes of freedom. You can't have more, or less,
> than me. And there is no temporary suspension of free-
> dom. Once on loan, you never get it back. Americans
> who think freedom is negotiable or malleable are, by
> our Founding Fathers' standards, not Americans.

In 2012 LaPierre cautioned NRA members against President Obama's election. "America as we know it will be on its
way to being lost forever." When Representative Gabrielle
Giffords was shot in 2011, along with others in Tucson, Ar-
izona, he said, "the acts of a deranged madman" could not
impede the rights of lawful citizens to bear arms. As LaPierre once wrote in a column for the NRA's in-house magazine, *American Rifleman*, "When you're at war, you do what
it takes to win."

He knows this is the type of speech that works for the
NRA's core membership — rural Americans — and for many
whites in America. A 2016 Pew Research Center poll shows
that 61 percent of whites prefer gun rights to gun control.
In comparison, just 31 percent of blacks prefer gun rights
to gun control. The problem for the NRA is that the country is becoming more urban and less rural. Some cities have

experienced bumps in growth larger than 10 percent in recent years, and 59 percent of folks who live in urban areas want more gun control. These numbers are also tied to education: 55 percent of Americans with a college degree favor more gun control. As we grow more diverse and more educated as a nation, the NRA continues to play to its base. It refuses to acknowledge black men like me except in dogwhistle terms, and that can have unforeseen consequences — such as the creation of a black version of the NRA.

. . . .
. . . .
. . . .
. . . .
. . . .

9

BLACK NRA

THE OUTCRY WAS heard across the nation after thirty-two-year-old Philando Castile, yet another black man, was shot and killed by police officer Jeronimo Yanez of St. Anthony, Minnesota. Castile was licensed to carry the concealed firearm in his possession on July 6, 2016, when Officer Yanez pulled him over in Falcon Heights, Minnesota. Castile alerted Yanez to his concealed gun and was reaching for his driver's license during what should've been a routine traffic stop over a busted taillight. When the officer told him not to move, Castile put his hands up, and Yanez shot him dead. We know this only because Castile's girlfriend had the presence of mind to broadcast her lover's death live on Facebook. The media storm to follow covered everything from marchers chanting in the street to a statement from Minnesota's governor: "Nobody should be shot and killed in Minnesota . . . for a tail light being out of function. Nobody should be shot and killed while seated still in their car. I'm heartbroken." The nation was in an uproar, and everyone had something to say — except the leadership of the NRA.

Many, including some rank-and-file members of the NRA, demanded to know why this had happened. This tragedy involved what the NRA would normally call a gross infringement of constitutional rights, yet its leadership did not publicly condemn Yanez's actions. In fact, the NRA took its sweet time responding in any way to Castile's death. Nearly thirty-six hours passed before the nation's fiercest defender of gun rights released a statement on its Facebook page. It neither named Castile nor took up what many believed would be the predictable stance: defending Castile's right to not be shot simply for legally possessing a firearm.

"As the nation's largest and oldest civil rights organization," the NRA's post read, "the NRA proudly supports the right of law-abiding Americans to carry firearms for defense of themselves and others regardless of race, religion, or sexual orientation. The reports from Minnesota are troubling and must be thoroughly investigated. In the meantime, it is important for the NRA not to comment while the investigation is ongoing. Rest assured, the NRA will have more to say once all the facts are known."

The only thing I was assured of, in the aftermath of Castile's shooting, was how truly indifferent the NRA is to the lives of black men when they exercise their rights as law-abiding citizens. But I also read posts by NRA members uniquely perturbed that the association had not stood for Castile when he could not stand for himself.

"Your lack of message concerning the Castile case disappoints me and makes me question my membership," a fella named Marco Gallologic posted on the NRA's Facebook page. Another named Brad Groux tweeted at the NRA's handle: "As a life member, please condemn the murder of Philando Castile, sooner rather than later. Licensed to carry, and no felony record."

These were just two of the voices in a small deluge following the death of Castile, calling out the suddenly muted mouth of the NRA.

It is, after all, an organization that prides itself on its bark. The NRA contributed $1,087,700 to political campaigns in the 2016 election cycle, spent $3,188,000 on lobbying efforts, and accounted for $54,747,518 in outside spending to promote the NRA's mission. The NRA spokeswoman and conservative talk radio host Dana Loesch epitomized that NRA bark in a 2017 NRA ad, "Violence of Lies," which incites aggression and calls for armed resistance.

"They use their media to assassinate real news," Loesch said.

> *They use their schools to teach children that their president is another Hitler. They use their movie stars and singers and award shows to repeat their narrative over and over again. And then they use their ex-president to endorse the resistance. All to make them march, make*

> *them protest, make them scream racism and sexism*
> *and xenophobia and homophobia and smash win-*
> *dows, burn cars, shut down interstates and airports,*
> *bully and terrorize the law abiding — until the only*
> *option left is for the police to do their jobs and stop the*
> *madness. And when that happens, they'll use it as an*
> *excuse for their outrage. The only way we stop this, the*
> *only way we save our country and our freedom is to*
> *fight this violence of lies with the clenched fist of truth.*

Ads like this position people who look like me, or who supported President Barack Obama, as nefarious monsters, when the truth is, we are terrified of the people who believe the hateful rhetoric that Loesch spews. The Southern Poverty Law Center documented 867 incidents of hateful harassment in the ten days following Election Day 2016. Among them, 280 incidents were categorized as anti-immigrant, while 187 were categorized as antiblack. The kind of people who made and are receptive to hateful NRA rhetoric are the ones I believe might kill me because I am a black man. The "Violence of Lies" ad does not merely pit *us* against *them*. It comes dangerously close to equating the right of public protest to treachery and to recommending police violence. And it falls right in line with the NRA zeitgeist: *Scared of someone? Shoot him. Don't understand someone? Shoot him too.* But the shame isn't simply in the NRA's inflammatory ads or rhetoric. The shame is in how willing we are to allow its ridiculous, dangerous language to distract us from facts.

NRA surrogates are quick to mention their two black board members — the army lieutenant colonel and former US representative Allen West, and the NBA hall-of-famer Karl Malone. The rock star Ted Nugent also serves on the NRA's board, and in 2014, he wrote this Facebook post for his more than three million followers:

> *Don't let your kids growup [sic] to be thugs who think they can steal, assault & attack cops as a way of life & badge of black (dis)honor. Don't preach your racist bullshit "no justice no peace" as blabbered by Obama's racist Czar Al Not So Sharpton & their black klansmen [sic]. When a cop tells you to get out of the middle of the street, obey him & don't attack him as brainwashed by the gangsta [sic] assholes you hang with & look up to. It's that simple unless you have no brains, no soul, no sense of decency whatsoever. And dont [sic] claim that "black lives matter" when you ignore the millions you abort & slaughter each & every day by other blacks. Those of us with a soul do indeed believe black lives matter, as all lives matter. So quit killin [sic] each other you fuckin idiots.*

With its hardline conservative politics, compounded by rhetoric like this coming from a board member, the NRA has quite an image problem with liberal-leaning minority

Americans. After all, the NRA threw its robust lobbying efforts behind a presidential candidate who also received support from alt-right groups, white nationalists, and hate groups, including the Ku Klux Klan.

The NRA knows it has a minorities problem, and has made recent attempts to recruit more black members.

But it is hard to take a man like the NRA commentator Colion Noir seriously on this score. In a photo for the *Los Angeles Times,* Noir, a black man, can be seen wearing a New York Yankees baseball cap, a black V-neck T-shirt, ripped blue jeans, and red-and-white Jordans. Also in the photo? Noir's matte-black assault rifle, tucked between his legs — a large phallus. Noir owns a law degree from Texas Southern University's Thurgood Marshall School of Law, a Glock 17, and a custom AR-15. He's used to being called a token for the NRA as well as an Uncle Tom by blacks. Propping up Noir as the NRA's black ideal counts for fuck-all, given the larger context.

Still, because there is money left on the table — blacks own guns at only half the rate (15 percent) as whites (31 percent) — it's no coincidence that the NRA's annual national convention of 2017 was held in Atlanta, Georgia, a gun-friendly state that boasts a large black population.

It's no coincidence, either, that a black alternative to the NRA has arisen. When the country's most powerful gun lobby is either late in commenting, not interested, or both, when a black man is gunned down while abiding by the law, it gives the rest of my country permission not to care what happens to me. It allows Americans to treat the killing of upstanding citizens as normal — as long as they are black.

This thinking has, more than anything else, led to more black men and women arming themselves: No one will protect us. So we must protect ourselves.

THE NATIONAL AFRICAN-AMERICAN Gun Association (NAAGA), which bills itself as welcoming to all "religious, social, and racial perspectives," was founded on February 28, 2015, by its president, Philip Smith. Smith has said he would like to see the group reach a membership of 250,000. Yet Smith hadn't even been introduced to guns until well after he'd graduated from college: "The only time I saw a gun was on TV or with a police officer walking down the street." NAAGA began as a way to honor Black History Month, according to Smith. "Our organization is working hard to show that we are law-abiding citizens just like everyone else," Smith said. "We have families. We work. We care about politics and enjoy sports and want to have a gun to protect ourselves and our families."

After three years, the organization boasts forty-seven chapters in twenty-six states. NAAGA's membership saw a jump during the lead-up to, and following, the 2016 election. Between November 2015 and February 2016, the association added 4,285 members. During the same time span a year later, it added 9,000. NAAGA offers membership at $29 annually, although no one has yet been turned away for not being able to pay. "There's nothing hidden, nobody's funding us, the NRA or the Democratic party or the Republican party . . . nobody owns us," says Smith.

Perks of membership include a membership card, access to NAAGA's monthly newsletter, voting participation in local chapter meetings, invitations to gun-safety courses, and discounts on firearms, training, and shooting events. The total membership of NAAGA numbers more than twenty thousand. Other newly formed groups of black gun owners, like the New Black Panthers Party for Self-Defense and the Huey P. Newton Gun Club, are also pulling in numbers. "A lot of African American gun owners don't go to the range and we hope, as NAAGA continues to grow, that they will feel comfortable visiting ranges and developing their marksmanship skills," Smith said. "This is why the group was developed, to give our community a path to get firearm training and education."

Smith insists the group's agenda is not unlike the NRA's. He wants to facilitate firearm instruction and safety while educating black Americans about exercising a Second Amendment right that had once been stripped from them. "I'd be lying to you if I didn't say there's an apprehension in the community based on some of the political rhetoric, regardless if you're a Republican or Democrat, left or right," Smith said. "A lot of folks are just concerned with the way the country's being run right now."

Douglas Jefferson, NAAGA's media content director, is more blunt. "When it comes down to it, it doesn't matter whether or not our people are armed, because that's not the weapon some people are afraid of. Our blackness is the weapon. That's what they're afraid of."

Since he cannot take that moment when a white person might pull a gun on him to educate or inform, he's preparing for what might be the worst day of his life: the day he might have to shoot a person in self-defense.

Doug Jefferson's fear is my fear too. Except I have chosen to remove the option of shooting someone in self-defense from my toolbox. There's no difference between NAAGA and the NRA in that respect. Both associations advocate shooting back. And I will not.

JEFFERSON CHOSE TO attend the NRA convention in Atlanta in 2017 because the NRA is the biggest and best there is today at defending and advocating for the Second Amendment and at instituting training programs. "I give them props on that. Outside of that, as far as political stances, there's a lot that me and the NRA are not going to agree with. Much of what they represent is not in line with my politics." Jefferson became an NRA member while at the convention. He had resisted joining until he saw the NRA offered a means for him to pursue many of his personal goals. Jefferson plans to become an NRA-certified instructor, and then, once he achieves certification, he'll let the membership go. "Across the board, everyone I talked to with knowledge of firearms training pointed me to the NRA's courses," he said. "It's a baseline for proficiency. So I've had to compartmentalize my beliefs and the NRA's [politics] for my own personal and professional goals." The NRA makes its courses much cheaper for its members and has discount programs in place with gun ranges, stores, and manufacturers. From a purely economic standpoint, if you're a gun enthusiast, it makes sense to be an NRA member.

Jefferson lives in Atlanta, in one of the most gun-friendly states in America. He shoots often at Stoddard's Range and Guns in Atlanta when not working in security at Hartsfield-Jackson Atlanta International Airport.

He began shooting a decade ago at the encouragement of friends while employed by the Georgia Department of Defense. Some of the men he worked with were veterans. Upon finding out that Doug had never shot a gun, a few made it their personal task to get him to a range.

"I was like, OK, 'I kind of like this,'" he said. "I tried a couple of handguns. Tried out an AR-15. Instantly fell in love with it. This is great. This is fun stuff. Then I saved my pennies up and went to the gun store and was like, Yeah, I'll take that one on the wall. Bought it, and that's how it started."

The rifle was a Bushmaster AR-15. Jefferson shot it for about two months before he bought and sold a couple more assault rifles. Slowly, he began to see shooting as more than a hobby. He began to see it as a form of self-defense. That's when he decided it was time to purchase a handgun. He didn't spend a lot of time shopping around. He bought a Glock 19.

"I had to," he said. "I literally live five minutes from the Glock factory. I can throw a rock into Smyrna. They're like the Honda Civics of handguns. [The Glock is] not real flashy, but it works, it's reliable, it's got everything you need."

Jefferson began practicing with the pistol almost immediately, knowing he was going to conceal-carry. But he wasn't practicing to gain a handgun license. Georgia residents don't have to have any firearm training, safety courses, or qualification to obtain a handgun license. "The turnaround — they tell you it will be thirty days," he said, "but it was way shorter than thirty days. It took all of two weeks, to the day. You go to the probate court to fill the application out, take your photograph, write your check, and then you go home. Two weeks later it comes in the mail."

Jefferson is becoming more proficient with firearms because he fears what might occur if he doesn't. He recognizes that crime happens everywhere, and that its frequency depends as much upon geography as socioeconomic demographics.

"White people are victims of black criminals. Black people are victims of black criminals," he says. "But there is also a history of black people being victims of racist white violence. And me living in a state where a lot of that has taken place in the past, it would just be irresponsible to not own a firearm, train with it, and prepare for a situation. I hope and pray it never happens to me or a loved one, but I don't have the luxury of making that decision. The other guy gets a say. I need to be prepared if the other guy puts that say into action."

He fears the implicit bias of white people — those who see us and think we want to hurt them.

I WAS SITTING at Barnes & Noble on a Sunday when I heard Sondra Stidham Holt's name called from the coffee shop. I'd seen her walk in, but this was our first meeting, and I had only her Facebook profile picture as a way to identify her. I'd wanted to be sure it was her before speaking.

"Sondra?"

She cocked her head and smiled at me. "RJ, right?"

I showed her to my table and was about to sit in the chair facing the door when she stopped me.

"Do you mind?" She motioned to the chair I had chosen.

I shook my head. "Not at all."

"You got muscles. You'll be OK."

This was a nod to a mutual understanding. We both lived in the same world — the same reality. But I am a man, and I do not worry about all forms of assault — a privilege she will never experience. Still, we both occupied a space where we do not always feel safe and must take precautions. Anybody could come through the front door of that bookstore and decide to make this day our worst ever.

I learned Sondra has held a concealed-carry license in Oklahoma since 2009. She carries a .22 pistol when she's out running errands and a Glock 42 when she feels shit could get real. Her hair is twisted into beautiful dark dreadlocks on one side of her head, with the other side shaved. Her nails are painted copper and silver and laced with glitter. When I asked her if she was carrying a gun, she chastised herself.

"Today I've been kind of lazy because it's Sunday," she said. "And I shouldn't be. Today is exactly the kind of day I should be more vigilant. Just because everybody just got out of church doesn't mean they were in church hearing the sermon." She carries her gun most days, always after dark; she never sits with her back to the door, and loves to tell stories.

"This Christian, you see I'm using air quotes around *Christian*," Sondra said, "dude was like, *Oh you carry a gun? You must be crazy.* Please, you carrying a Bible for protection — instead of a gun. Who's the crazy person here?" Sondra told another story about a woman contemplating carrying a gun, but only if it was a girly gun — pink-colored. This, Sondra could not abide. "Irks the shit out of me," she said. "Like who's gon' stop because your gun is pink? 'Oh, you got a pink gun. I'm not gonna hurt you.' Who cares? Does it have bullets? Does it shoot? That's the shit to care about."

Sondra had watched as a coworker, a woman, at her job was continually sexually harassed by another coworker, a man. She watched as this man became so devious and physical with his harassment that Sondra feared for the woman and told her to get a gun. "I don't think you have to be just like 'rah-rah feminism' to carry a gun," she said. "I just think you should have it in case something happens. But [my coworker] felt like she couldn't say anything. She felt too scared to say anything. I think knowing how to use a gun, knowing what it's for, would've helped her feel safe telling that dude to quit it. I don't feel like I'll get sexually harassed less, but if a guy knows I might have a gun, he might not say anything at all."

In 2001, only 6.6 percent of American women owned a handgun. That's fewer than one in ten. But for every incident in which a woman used a handgun in self-defense in 1998, 101 women were murdered with a handgun. Just over a decade later, things had hardly changed for black women. In 2009, black women were murdered at more than twice the rate of white women. Today, black women are the fastest-growing demographic among concealed-carry handgun licensees. Though no group keeps track of gun sales according to race, Kevin Jones, the director of the Ohio chapter of NAAGA and the former owner of Urban Sports Limited, said he saw "about a three- to four-fold increase in African-Americans coming to his shop to buy firearms. Most of them are black women."

Black women like Sondra are so fearful for their well-being that they have purchased guns. Sondra had a bad scare twenty years earlier when a Georgia Tech football player kicked the door of the apartment she shared with roommates. "We had a rule," Sondra said. "If you ain't in our apartment by 1 a.m., you ain't coming in. I don't care who you are." The roommates all adhered to that rule. So when Sondra's roommate's ex-boyfriend knocked on the door "like nobody's business, like he was the police or something," they weren't about to open it. He was mad that one of the women had broken up with him, felt he'd been cheated on, and his approach to illustrating his frustration left the roommates cowering in the back of the apartment. He kicked in the door, yelling and throwing things.

Sondra's roommate tried talking with her ex, but he grew only louder, angrier. This led Sondra's second roommate to retrieve a gun her father had given her. She brought it into the living room. It didn't matter that the gun was not loaded. When the ex-boyfriend saw it, he immediately calmed. He even asked her not to shoot him and left quickly. They decided not to call the police because, despite the incident, they didn't want to relive this violent experience.

"When my dad found out," Sondra said, "he was like, *We not playing this game.* He was not thrilled about that at all." She was twenty-four when he gave her the .22 pistol she still carries today. "It kind of made that light bulb turn on for us," Sondra said. "We felt pretty secure where we were. But here's this guy, a football player for Georgia Tech, breaking in, essentially, to hurt somebody. It woke us up. This dude kicked in the door, and we could've all been hurt." She's carried a gun most days for twenty-one years now, and she doesn't see why other women don't. "For all intents and purposes for me, you should. Because of threats. There's subtle feminine threats that you get. There's subtle political threats that you get. You should just be armed and know."

NO ONE KEEPS statistics on gun sales by race. Firearms dealers across the country have, however, reported a rise in black folks buying guns. A 2017 Pew Research Center poll found 49 percent of white households, compared to 32 percent of black households, had one or more guns. The same poll found that 49 percent of all black Americans see the immediate threat of gun violence against them as a "very big" problem. Couple these polled opinions with the knowledge that 57 percent of black folks know someone who has been shot. It's little wonder that a group like the National African American Gun Association took root and grew exponentially a mere three months after the 2016 election.

10

YOU'RE WORTH MORE TO ME, ASSHOLE

HE WAS LOUD and arrogant, and he carried his sidearm in plain view while talking about the way things once were in his country, when it was apparently an idyllic if overpopulated Mayberry. So I'll call him Barney Fife.

I was standing in Barney Fife's apartment in the part of southwest Oklahoma City that rich white people tend to avoid when he launched into his soliloquy. There are more than 310 million guns in circulation in the United States — a gun for every man, woman, and child. Gun owners outnumber local, state, and federal law enforcement seventy-nine to one. All reasons why my about-to-be gun dealer, who was federally licensed and legal, was moaning about the flooded market. The market had forced him and his ilk to drop their prices, and it was beginning to hurt his bottom line. "What we need," he said, "is another wacko with an assault rifle — that'll send a run on."

The insensitivity and hate of that statement hit me full-force. But even I know you don't pick a fight with a man who has an AR-15 lying on his coffee table and a hand cannon strapped to his thigh, like Samuel L. Jackson in the only cop movie I like. Besides, I needed this man. I'd bought my Glock 17 online through a firearms forum with nothing but a debit card. That got me a sheet of paper that directed me to pick up the gun from a federally licensed dealer. Which is where Barney Fife came in. I signed my name, refused to shake his hand, and continued to wonder what I was missing about most gun owners' view of the world. Why didn't they believe the physics of what carrying a gun can and can't save you from, or the statistics related to accidental and unjustified gun killings in our surreally gun-overwhelmed country? And why were they so much more likely to pull a gun on me than on someone who looked like them?

I HAD CONTRACTED to buy my Glock 17 because I needed it — or any pistol with a full-size magazine — to complete the requirements of becoming a Self Defense Act Instructor in the state of Oklahoma. The instructor course lasts at least sixteen hours and must be administered by a professional organization recognized by the Council on Law Enforcement Education and Training. The NRA is on the list. I decided to use the nation's most powerful defender of the Second Amendment for my two days of instruction.

By this time, I had spent a lot of time learning to fire my Glock 26 with the kind of proficiency that garnered attention from onlookers at my local gun range — the same range where Waldo had trained me. I had a routine. I practiced with purpose, and I did not deviate from it. Not for the white men who spat at my feet as they went by my stall. Not for the man who faked shooting a jump shot at me as he went by. Not on the days when I felt I was practicing without improving. Most folks wouldn't even mention that I was shooting well for a black guy, which has happened on four occasions as of this writing. Overt racism at my gun range, and every other gun range I have visited, isn't common. I've found most people keep to themselves. Like I imagine most people do at peep shows. It's just the supremely hateful and supremely ignorant who say such things.

OUTSIDE THE RANGE — during those two years I spent shooting to get closer to Charles, shooting to exercise my Second Amendment right as a historically literate black man, but increasingly shooting to get better at it than any fucking asshole — the presence of guns never left me. I saw NO GUNS decals plastered on doors outside the movie theaters, restaurants, and grocery stores that I frequented, and even at my gym. I found myself staring at the middle-aged white man in jeans, New Balance tennis shoes, and a Sooner shirt while he paid for his coffee at 7-Eleven. The bulge beneath his shirt, right above his hip, looked cancerous, a malignant tumor aching to be cut away. When he reached forward to hand the cashier his money, I saw the flash of a pistol grip. I didn't turn away quickly enough. The man caught me staring and aggressively pulled down his shirt to cover up what he must have known wasn't a secret.

THE LOCKERS AT my gym are usually closed, usually locked. On this day, one wasn't. I did not find it funny to discover that a short, small black pistol had been left there. Why had it been left for me to see? And what should I do? Should I tell the teenage girl at the front desk what I'd seen, only to frighten her, or worse, to find out she wasn't frightened at all? Should I guard the open locker? Make sure the only person who got to it was the person who was supposed to?

He stepped in front of me. If I had been in line, it would've seemed as if he'd cut in. He was fully clothed and combing his hair. He dropped the comb in the locker, pulled out the pistol, and shoved it into a small holster, which sat just inside his waistband, two fingers to the right of the belt buckle. He flipped on his jacket, grabbed his gym bag, and walked away. For him, I don't think I was ever there.

I NEEDED TO buy new tennis shoes. That's why I was wandering around Academy Sports; wandering is what you do in a box store. That's how I found myself in the part of the sporting-goods store for killing defenseless animals.

There were bows and arrows and knives and all manner of hunting accessories to purchase. There were rifles. And there were handguns. Also ammunition — a lot of ammunition. Towering several feet above me, the shelves made the place look more like an armory than a sportsman's sanctuary. The number of different calibers, grains, casings, and brands was overwhelming—Hornady Critical Duty Flex-Lock .45 Auto +P 220-Grain Handgun, Winchester Super X 20-Gauge Game Loads 7.5 Shotshells . . . and what the hell was Fiocchi Pistol Shooting Dynamics 9 mm Jacketed Hollow-Point Centerfire Handgun Ammunition?

I took out my phone and Googled "jacketed hollow-point." I learned quickly that a hollow-point bullet is, well, hollowed out, or pitted, at the tip. This so the bullet will expand, explode, and shatter once it hits its target. I learned that this bullet is favored by people who carry concealed weapons for self-defense because of the greater damage it can do.

Because, apparently, regular bullets fired from a gun aren't lethal enough already.

I looked up from my phone to stare at the box of jacketed hollow-point rounds. What was I missing? Why was a bullet like this enough in demand to be sold at a sporting-goods store that also featured kids shoes? Then it dawned on me. Anyone who buys these bullets is someone who is willing to kill, who might want to kill. George Zimmerman used a small lightweight pistol made specifically for self-defense, a Kel-Tec 9 mm PF-9, to shoot through the heart and kill Trayvon Martin—an unarmed black child with twenty-two dollars, earbuds, and Skittles in his pocket—with a hollow-point round in a Sanford, Florida, townhouse complex at 7:17 p.m. on February 26, 2012. Zimmerman would later claim he was in fear for his life.

· · · · ·

SIX OF THE nine people in my class at the Oklahoma City Gun Range, in Arcadia, were members of the Oklahoma City Police Department. Of the three of us who were not affiliated with OKC PD, one was an out-of-work information technology professional and the other was the instructor's sixteen-year-old kid. The NRA has a program for girls and boys age thirteen and older who want to become "apprentice instructors," at the bottom third of the three tiers in the NRA's pyramid of instructors. The second tier, the one I was going for, is basic instructor. The third is NRA training counselor, who teaches the first and second tiers how to teach. Our counselor for the occasion was a former army sergeant, current OKC PD sergeant, and Boy Scout scoutmaster, with a face permanently fixed in what looked to me like a snarl.

In a small class, you might think it would be easy for me to get comfortable. But being surrounded by law enforcement made me feel as I do whenever I'm pulled over — anxious and severely marginalized. Only this time, the pull-over-license-and-registration-please-are-there-any-drugs-in-the-car would last sixteen hours, with no dash-cam footage. We went around the room, stating who we were and why we wanted to become instructors. When my turn approached, that feeling magnified.

I blurted out that I wanted to better understand why gun owners feel the need to carry a gun or keep a gun. The room didn't go silent, like it does in the movies. Instead, the IT guy rather quickly asked me if I knew that this class was for those who wanted to *teach* proper firearm safety and use. I said I did, but I believed that part of effective teaching had to do with the curriculum. What biases might be reflected in the NRA course structure? Who was doing the teaching, and might they bring their own biases to the table? Where and to whom were most concealed-carry classes taught? I'd hoped to get to know a few of them and hear their stories as they became instructors themselves.

But Bertrand Russell taught us hope is born of misery.

During a break, one of the police officers — I'll call him George Washington, to suggest a character reeking of machismo, white privilege, and tobacco — found me outside the classroom. We stood there for a while. I was checking my phone while he finished a cigarette. I'm sure it couldn't have been longer than five minutes, but it felt longer. It felt surreally heavy. In fact, that's mostly how my notes from that day read, like a deranged fever dream. But I managed to get this down because, well, it struck me as especially important.

As if the words burst forth out of some sincere need, George Washington said, "I know what you're *doing*."

"I'm sorry?"

George Washington looked irritated now. "I know what you're doing. You're gonna teach them to shoot *back*."

To which I said — nothing. I'd like to believe that my face was a potent concoction of contempt and disbelief, but only George Washington could tell you for sure. He stared back at me long enough to make me feel genuinely confused. Then he walked back inside.

. . . . .

AFTER SHOWING HOW to properly load and unload a single- and double-action revolver and semiautomatic pistol, clear a failure to fire and double feed, and then teach those skills, my classmates and I needed to show we could shoot worth a damn. For this NRA instructor certification, that meant putting eight out of ten shots into a grouping no wider than a dollar bill's length and no narrower than a dollar bill's width, from fifteen yards out — twice.

We took our positions on the range, put our ear-gear on, and waited for the command to fire. I took my time sighting in my target and letting the blast from the pistol surprise me. I treated each shot as its own and kept to my ritual.

Feet shoulder width apart.

Loose through the torso.

Arms comfortably extended.

Grip tight enough to feel in control.

Sight the target.

Align the sights.

Squeeze.

CHARLES WAS SITTING in his recliner in the living room. I marched in with my qualifying target in tow. It waved beside me as I walked through his house. I must have been smiling because my grin was the first thing Charles commented on.

"What for, though?" he asked.

I presented him my target. He stood, and took the target from me like it was his grandma's china. He examined it thoughtfully, and told me how proud of me he was. Charles had been my father-in-law for two years.

"You done good," he said.

This was the last time Charles would ever be proud of me. Wish I'd hugged him then. Wish I'd told him how much I will always love his daughter. Wish I'd told him how much I love him.

I'M LOOKING AT my certificate now. Even a year after receiving it, it still shocks the shit out of me. The signature of the NRA's secretary, John C. Frazier, appears in the bottom right corner, and a big NRA INSTRUCTOR insignia is at the bottom left. In the center, it says:

> *The National Rifle Association of America certifies that RJ YOUNG has successfully met the requirements set by the National Rifle Association of America and is hereby designated an NRA INSTRUCTOR and is authorized to teach the following basic courses: Certified Pistol.*

So it's there. This is the proof. This means that all the rounds I've shot, the skill as a marksman I've gained, and the experience of safely storing and transporting a pistol I've earned have made me an expert with a handgun.

If you're an asshole, I shoot better than you.

If you're an asshole, I will not shoot you.

Because you're worth more to me, asshole.

11

. . . .
. . . .
. . . .
. . . .
. . . .

SELF-DEFENSE IN BLACK AND WHITE

THE NRA'S HAND on the lucrative lever of reinforcing white contempt and fear of black men is at least well out in the open for anyone willing to look. But my descent into the rabbit hole of gun culture revealed the presence of a national industry I never had imagined, one with a mission I wish I could forget.

ON NOVEMBER 14, 2007, a Texas resident, Joe Horn, called the 911 dispatcher. The sixty-one-year-old made his intent clear.

"I've got a shotgun," Horn said. "Do you want me to stop them?"

"Nope, don't do that," the dispatcher said. "No property worth shooting somebody over, OK?"

This upset Horn. He didn't like the idea of having to sit by while his house was burgled, and he had a means to put an end to the situation. After all, he knew the law. "I have a right to protect myself," Horn said. "I ain't gonna let them get away with this shit. I'm sorry, this ain't right, buddy . . . They got a bag of loot . . . Here it goes, buddy. You hear the shotgun clicking, and I'm going."

He confronted the burglars. "Move, you're dead." Then he shot three times and killed both burglars.

Horn returned to the dispatcher. "I had no choice, they came in the front yard with me, man, I had no choice."

A grand jury found Horn had not committed a crime, but not before legal fees took their toll on him. Gun enthusiasts took this as a warning. That a man could be defending his property, shoot two Colombian burglars who were in the country illegally, and still end up destitute did not seem right to them. U.S. Law Shield, an organization dedicated to providing legal representation for its members, if ever they are called upon to defend their lives, their family, or their property by using a firearm or any lawful weapon, was founded by two Texas lawyers, Darren Rice and T. Edwin Walker, in part as a response to the furor over the Horn case. No gun owner wants to end up broke for doing what he or she believes is right.

I FIRST LEARNED of U.S. Law Shield when a representative of the organization made a pitch to my concealed-carry class. Waldo had introduced the rep, a middle-aged white guy in a gray suit and button-down shirt, who asked what we were going to do when we had to "put a man down because he attacks you or your loved ones." How were we going to navigate the legality of the situation from the moment we called 911 to the day we had to stand before the magistrate and answer for our actions? Turns out U.S. Law Shield provides a hotline, making civil and criminal attorneys available to all members of U.S. Law Shield, twenty-four hours a day, seven days a week, 365 days a year. I learned that you don't actually have to use a firearm to receive legal services under the program. You can simply brandish your gun — to stop a threat, of course. A base package for a married couple would cost just $240.

U.S. Law Shield, with over 200,000 members, is not the only organization in the country that provides this kind of service. There are dozens, and they're all perfectly fine with the idea of increasing the numbers of people inclined to pull out a gun to resolve a problem.

In 2017, the NRA announced it would form its own firearms legal service program, called NRA Carry Guard. Another organization under the NRA's umbrella is Second Call Defense, which will, in addition to delivering legal services, retrieve or replace the gun you used to (we hope not) kill a person when it has been taken into custody by police; provide expert witness coordination; and make available a personal crisis manager. To complement its legal services programs, the NRA looks to fortify its place among those competing in the firearm self-defense market by offering a concealed-carry training component for the folks who think a lot about when and how they might need to shoot in self-defense. The NRA enlisted the help of the Navy SEALs' George Severence and Eric Frohardt as well as the Green Berets' James R. Jarrett and Jeff Houston to lead the association's national instructor-certification team. An organization called the United States Concealed Carry Association performs many of the same services that U.S. Law Shield does, including providing an attorney, money for bail, and a wallet card with instructions for exactly what to do after you shoot and kill a person in self-defense. The USCCA's most expensive package costs $30 a month and provides up to $125,000 for the cost of a criminal attorney and up to $1 million for civil damages incurred.

"This is basically preparing people: you're going to kill someone, and you need to know what to do," says Mary Anne Franks, a professor of law at the University of Miami.

When U.S. Law Shield pitched its services at my concealed-carry class, where everyone but me was white and barely knew how to shoot a gun, this was the presenter's clincher: What if we were George Zimmerman? Just trying to be a good citizen and protect our neighborhood? This was two years after Zimmerman had shot and killed Trayvon Martin. I felt my legs clutch, a signal for me to please not lose my shit. The man broke from his speech for a moment, as his eyes settled on me. But he was quick to pick up with his practiced delivery. He knew he'd lost me. He knew he never had a chance to sell me. So why waste effort on me? Why indeed.

This apathy is the emotion I hate most. It makes me angriest and most fearful. If this man, intent on demonstrating to our class the importance of his services, chooses to make his case by citing an incident that half the country believes was a murder — if he doesn't have the sensitivity to see me in the room and choose a different example, it shows that he doesn't believe I'm worth the effort. So why would anyone else who believes what he believes try to engage with me in a positive way? How do I begin a dialogue with a person like that? How do I convince him that my fears are real, and that he directly contributes to them?

I ATTENDED A gun-law workshop put on by U.S. Law Shield of Oklahoma three miles from my apartment in Tulsa, soon after I earned my NRA instructor certification. There's a difference I need to point out here: taking a U.S. Law Shield class as an NRA certified expert is not the same as taking the class as a budding intermediate shooter learning his way around a gun. Suffice it to say: I attended the class to call bullshit.

This being Tulsa, I was not surprised to find that I and one other person, a woman, were the only black people in a room of thirty. When I first arrived, I overheard an older man ask how much the workshop would cost. He was pleased to find out it was free. All we needed to do was sign in with our name and email address, enjoy the cookies and Cokes set out for us, and listen. I took a seat at the front of the room, facing a table that displayed a large U.S. Law Shield poster. I listened to chatter about the gun raffle advertised as part of the workshop itself. Turns out this was the reason many had come — the hope of getting a free handgun.

On its website, U.S. Law Shield advertises many events across the country just like the one I was attending. The legal-defense program was so enthusiastically received in Texas that its founding lawyers decided to take the program national, setting up organizations in Florida, Oklahoma, Colorado, Pennsylvania, Missouri, Georgia, Virginia, New Jersey, Ohio, Arkansas, and Kansas.

As I waited, I picked up a brochure. It featured a white man in a suit and tie, holding the kind of placard you've seen in mug shots. Where a name usually appears, there was the legend LEGAL GUN OWNER. Above the picture was written "Criminal or victim? If you own a gun, it can happen to you."

Inside, the brochure listed ten categories of scenarios that U.S. Law Shield has encountered in its role as a "firearms defense legal defense program."

- Member shot robbers at family business.
- Member shot late-night intruder. Civil lawsuit followed.
- Member brought to grand jury after using gun to stop intruder in own home.
- Member arrested for legally carrying a gun on own property.

- Thief attempted to run over member with stolen truck. Member shoots and kills.

- Member shot rabid dog on own property — wrongfully issued criminal citation.

- Member victim of off-duty police officer's misunderstanding of law — arrested for legal gun.

- Member forced to shoot carjacker. Member victim of road-rage incident — arrested for defending self.

I am not aware of any cases involving U.S. Law Shield members who are black.

The voice of Kirk Evans, a Houston-area attorney who has been a member of the Texas Bar since 1993 and is currently president of the organization, is the one I heard on the membership services hotline, encouraging me to become a member. U.S. Law Shield employs "independent program attorneys" in every state. The organization's model has not, however, stood unchallenged.

A 2013 class-action lawsuit alleged that Texas Law Shield LLP engaged in barratry — commonly known as ambulance chasing. The plaintiffs, Brad and Terrilyn Crowley, alleged that a salesperson for Texas Law Shield was pitching to students at a concealed-carry class, encouraging them to sign on to Texas Law Shield at a cost of about $130 a year, for peace of mind. "In return, so the sales pitch goes, Texas Law Shield will provide legal advice to all clients and a legal defense, with no additional charge, to any client who is civilly sued or criminally charged as a result of using a firearm so long as the member was using the firearm in a legally permissible location," according to a petition filed in *Brad Crowley v. Texas Law Shield.*

This is, as you've seen, exactly what happened to me in my concealed-carry class in Oklahoma. U.S. Law Shield's headquarters in Houston had no comment regarding the organization's policy related to pitching their firearm-defense program at concealed-carry classes.

Texas Law Shield and its sister program, U.S. Law Shield, are commonly misconstrued as law firms or insurance companies. They are not law firms. And Texas Law Shield is only a quasi insurance company. Texas Law Shield, made up of several limited liability corporations, has spread out over various states without in fact having a unified program.

Because most of the states in which U.S. Law Shield offers legal-service plans do not regulate the industry, the company can presumably stop defending a member at will, if, for instance, the state organization runs out of money.

Then there's this troubling clause, wherein Texas Law Shield defines the use of a firearm as

> *any incident where the Legal Service Contract Holder either discharges or displays a firearm for the purpose of using the firearm as a weapon to stop a threat, whether the Legal Service Contract Holder pulls the trigger and discharges the firearm or not. This term does not include taking the firearm to a location that*

is prohibited by federal, state, or local law, negligent
or unintended discharges, or negligent or unintended
displays.

This is truly problematic for a contract holder. At the heart of legal cases related to guns is the issue of whether a person was using the gun to stop something *perceived* as a threat. The clause allows latitude for Texas Law Shield to conclude that a client was not justified in using a weapon and thus is not eligible for coverage. The Houston attorney Mark Bennett says, "Texas Law Shield looks to me like a sucker's bet. You'd be better off making friends with a good criminal-defense lawyer, sending him a good bottle of bourbon now and then, rather than sending your money to a company that, in the highly unlikely event you get in trouble with your gun, might — or might not — provide you with a lawyer of unknown provenance."

Yet U.S. Law Shield persists in its fear-mongering. According to the company, for 90 percent of its members, the need to use deadly force arises at their homes or near their vehicles. In the company's estimation, the deck is stacked against gun owners because of the media and the legal system. The overwhelming financial burden of legal defense during criminal prosecution or a civil suit makes U.S. Law Shield an essential protective measure for gun owners.

THE REPRESENTATIVE FROM U.S. Law Shield was six feet tall. He wore a black button-down shirt, blue jeans, and an openly carried Sig Sauer .380 pistol. Before he started his spiel, he stated that no video recording or photography of any kind was allowed during the event. He then launched into stories about U.S. Law Shield members who had been protected by the company's services, followed by tales about those who wished they'd had them. He described the financial strain for even those gun owners who shoot and kill a person in lawful self-defense. For $10.95 a month, a bit more than the cost of a Netflix subscription, he assured us we could all be saved from monetary stress. Should we have to use a gun in self-defense, we would have access to legal representation for criminal or civil proceedings anywhere in Oklahoma and receive updates on firearm carry laws, as we were about to in this very workshop.

"Like the card says" — the representative pointed to a stack of cards on the table — "you defend your life. We defend your freedom."

The sales pitch was followed by the keynote address. A bearded man named Blake Hayes, wearing an ill-fitting pinstriped suit, delivered it. As an attorney at Hanson & Holmes law office in Tulsa, with a special interest in the use of deadly force, Hayes gave us a basic understanding of gun laws in Oklahoma. He explained succinctly that according to the Oklahoma Firearms Act of 1971, a person is justified in the use of deadly force if that person feels in imminent peril of great bodily harm or death. Following his rundown of the Oklahoma Self-Defense Act, Hayes outlined recent changes to concealed-carry law in Oklahoma.

In May 2017, Hayes explained, Governor Mary Fallin signed Senate Bill 397 into law, which permits handgun licensees to carry firearms on public buses. Senate Bill 35 now allows some men and women in the military to carry a firearm without a license. Chiefly this "Handgun Carry Military Exemption" means that eighteen-year-old veterans may receive a handgun license. To wit: they can get a handgun license, but they still can't buy a beer.

As of August 25, 2017, according to Bill 397, it remains illegal for a person to possess a gun on elementary or secondary school grounds, except that "a concealed or unconcealed weapon may be carried onto private school property or in any school bus or vehicle used by any private school for transportation of students or teachers by a person who is licensed pursuant to the Oklahoma Self-Defense Act, provided a policy has been adopted by the governing entity of the private school that authorizes the carrying and possession of a weapon on private school property or in any school bus or vehicle used by a private school."

"Now it's mostly courthouses, jails, and post offices where you can't conceal," Hayes said.

"But what about those 'guns banned' signs?" an older white man asked. "Do I have to leave my gun?"

"People can bar you from entry," Hayes said. "But the law you'd be breaking is trespassing. That's the law violated." In Oklahoma, trespassing carries a maximum fine of $1,500 and no jail time upon first offense. But Hayes was quick to add that a business owner could ask you to leave for having a gun on his or her property only if he or she *knew* you had a gun. "I'm not telling you to go around and violate the law. I'm telling you to conceal your gun."

Hayes said he didn't see anything wrong with the advice he was giving; he himself followed it. The man walks around, most of the time, with a piece in his trousers and a vigilante's logic at the forefront of his mind. Make no mistake, Hayes said, he loves the law. But, to his way of thinking, the law won't save you from a bad guy. "Until a business demonstrates it takes my safety and the safety of my family as personally as I do," Hayes told the crowd, "I'm not going to surrender my firearm." For this, he received mild applause and at least one "You're goddamn right!" from a fella wearing a hat that identified him as a Vietnam War veteran.

During this portion of the workshop, I heard Hayes answer questions that dealt, in part, with shooting an unarmed person in the back, concealed carrying while at work, and the legality of walking into a police station with a firearm. A grandfather, who said he walked his grandson to school and was "concerned about dogs as much as anything," asked about the ramifications of carrying a firearm at a public school. Hayes explained that it was best he leave the gun at home or in his vehicle.

Another woman raised her hand, and Hayes called on her. "What if I shoot a burglar in my house?"

"Then that falls under the Castle Doctrine," Hayes said.

The Castle Doctrine is a part of the Oklahoma Firearms

Act of 1971 that states: "The Legislature hereby recognizes that the citizens of the State of Oklahoma have a right to expect absolute safety within their own homes or places of business." Then there's this part: "A person who uses force . . . is justified in using such force and is immune from criminal prosecution and civil action for the use of such force."

Imagine me walking into your house uninvited, wearing a tie-dye shirt with a huge peace sign screen-printed on it, environmentally safe shorts on my legs, a pair of Chacos on my feet, and a large poster held above my head reading, DON'T SHOOT! I LOVE YOU! If you shot me dead and then claimed to police that you "have held a reasonable fear of imminent peril of death or great bodily harm," it is highly unlikely you'd be under threat of prosecution by any district attorney in Oklahoma. Twenty-four states have some variation of the Castle Doctrine as law.

In March 2017, a twenty-three-year-old Oklahoman put the Castle Doctrine into action.

ZACH PETERS WAS asleep at around noon in his parents' home in Broken Arrow, Oklahoma — a suburb of Tulsa — when he heard a noise. It was the kind of noise that provoked a fight-or-flight response. He retrieved his AR-15 assault rifle, walked into the kitchen, and fired at three intruders. One of them fled. Peters took that moment to race back to his bedroom and call 911. He began to explain what had just occurred.

"OK, sir, we're getting people out that way," the 911 dispatcher said. "And they attempted to break into your house and then you shot them. Correct?"

"Correct," Peters said. "They got into my house. Two of them are still in my house."

"OK, are they white males?"

"Um, I didn't really get a good look."

"OK, can you see them right now?"

"I shot two of them, and now I'm barricaded in my bedroom."

"You're barricaded in your bedroom?"

"Correct. Southeast corner. They broke in the back door. I can hear one of them talking."

"OK, what are they saying?"

"I can't hear them."

"OK, where were they shot?"

"Upper-body."

"Are you hurt sir?"

"No."

He told the dispatcher which landmarks to look for when they arrived. Peters was still armed while on the phone with the dispatcher.

"OK, sir," the dispatcher said momentarily, "my deputy is on scene. I'm going to need you to unarm yourself and put the gun away."

"As soon as you confirm the deputy is in the house, I'll unload the weapon."

"Just go ahead and keep the deputy, I'm sorry, keep your weapon on your bed and remain unarmed please, sir."

Peters killed all three intruders — the third was found lying dead in the driveway. One of the suspects was carrying a knife. The others carried brass knuckles.

The three intruders were later identified as teenage boys — sixteen, seventeen, and nineteen years old. A spokesman for the sheriff's department said that, at first glance, the event looked like self-defense. Prosecutors eventually agreed. A medical examiner's autopsy found Peters had shot two of the teenagers in the back. They were fleeing. Still, the Oklahoma Firearms Act of 1971 states that a person can "expect absolute safety" in their dwelling and that deadly use of force is legal if it occurs "in the process of unlawfully and forcefully entering or had unlawfully and forcibly entered." The law sets no limit on shooting people who are leaving, fleeing, or have their back to you under those circumstances. You can shoot. You can kill. And the law will uphold the murder you committed as self-defense. Peters did not face any charges for the triple homicide.

Hayes used this incident as a teaching moment for the workshop.

"You're supposed to be able to kill anybody who comes into your house, but three kids dead shocks the conscience for a lot of people," Hayes said. "So that's a real-life example that's ripped out of the headlines where you can show somebody, even if they're kids, even if they don't have guns, you can shoot them if they're in your house, and you will get away with it. Because this guy did."

The only thing Peters had done wrong, according to

Hayes, was talk too much. Hayes's advice would've been to hang up just as soon as the police knew there was a crime and the address where it had occurred.

"I have a belief that everybody needs a legal defense," he said, "but the best representation I can give our members is talking to them before something like that happens. So if I was to get up in the middle of the night and go defend one of our members, I would tell them the same thing I tell them in the class, which is, 'Hey, we're not going to make a statement tonight. If they want to arrest you, they can arrest you. We'll bail you out, and you're gonna go home.'"

A FEW WEEKS after the workshop, I met with Hayes at his law office. It was a Friday, and he was dressed in blue jeans, sneakers, and an olive drab shirt reading WOOBIES across the front. He made himself a cup of coffee as he began to tell me just how he came to make deadly force in self-defense a legal specialty of his.

Hayes grew up boxing. It was his dad's favorite sport, and one he took to more than any other. He boxed into his teens, when the Ultimate Fighting Championship debuted in 1993. That's when he saw a skinny Brazilian named Royce Gracie annihilate all other combatants with a form of martial art called jiu-jitsu. "Royce choked everybody out and beat them all up," Hayes said. "I was like, *Man, I need to learn that stuff because if someone does that to me, I'm in trouble.* I'd never seen that kind of stuff before." He began formally training in jiu-jitsu in 1997, has since earned his black belt, and owns a jiu-jitsu academy where he is also an instructor.

From a family with a military background, Hayes was exposed to guns as a means of hunting and self-protection early in life, but only as an adult did he begin to see a handgun as a basic component of survival in a world where men and women can and will do harm to you and yours.

"I don't care if you're Mike Tyson," he said. "A six-year-old kid could be twenty yards away from you and shoot you and kill you before you can get over there and punch him. That's just the way it is. If you're serious about self-defense, you have to be armed and you have to know how to use a firearm. Otherwise, if a bad guy has one, you're dead."

Slowly Hayes developed firearms skills as a complement to his abilities in hand-to-hand combat. He helped create a system of self-defense that he and several former servicemen, including members of the Green Berets, expert marksmen, and one Ultimate Fighting Championship veteran, sell to the public. The instructors put on self-defense seminars, teaching how to properly address threats that you believe could endanger your life. "But the hardest part is not pulling the trigger," Hayes said.

This is why he set his mind to becoming one of the leading experts on Oklahoma's Self-Defense Act. He wanted to understand, and then help his students understand, just what the law expects from them as handgun license holders, exercisers of the Second Amendment, and protectors of themselves and their loved ones. It's this mission that spurred him to attend a U.S. Law Shield seminar at a Tulsa gun range. It did not surprise me that a man with his background and education would soon be recruited into the organization. But I was curious as to why he said yes to being the man called in the middle of the night during one of the worst experiences of someone's life.

"I've seen people not only lose their life savings," Hayes said, "but lose their mom and dad's life savings, their friend's, their uncle's, whoever's life savings, trying to protect themselves from a frivolous lawsuit or against criminal charges that shouldn't have been filed. I have, frankly, more financial means than the average person, and I would hate to have to cough up the kind of money it would take. So I have that insurance myself because $10.95 is a drop in the bucket compared to whatever it might cost me if I ever had to use my gun."

"But could this insurance be construed as giving someone a way to commit murder legally?" I asked.

"As an attorney, I can only deal with the evidence as it is. I mean, if you committed murder, it's going to be pretty tough for me to prove otherwise, and all of those companies have a disclaimer that if you've obviously committed murder and you haven't used reasonable force, you're not going to get a defense . . . Now if it's your word against somebody who was there who says it didn't seem reasonable to them and it seems reasonable to you, then that's when you really need an attorney. Having a good attorney who has experience doing that is important."

"I think if you present a gun," Hayes said, "and you tell somebody, 'If you don't back off I'm gonna shoot you,' and they continue to come forward, I don't think there are many juries, especially around here, that would convict you. I try to tell people if you have enough standoff to do it, especially if there are witnesses around, to say as loud as you can, *I'm gonna fucking shoot you if you don't stop!* So that then everybody there will say he said he was gonna shoot him if he didn't stop, and the person charged forward anyway."

I found this interesting. I decided to see how far down this path it would be prudent to go. I presented Hayes with a hypothetical situation.

"So what if I say, 'You just threatened my life by brandishing a gun'?"

"Right!" he said. "I did just threaten your life because you threatened my life, and the only way that one of us does not get killed is if you stop doing whatever it is I just asked you to stop doing."

"Then I call the police to say that you threatened my life. The police show up and I say . . . ?"

"Frankly, if that happened, I would tell somebody to say I'm going to wait until I can speak to my attorney. Generally, in a situation like that they won't arrest you. They'll fill out a report and send it to the district attorney, and they'll decide whether or not you need to be arrested. They'll take your gun and put it in evidence because it is evidence."

I told Hayes that, as a black man, this particular scenario frightens me for many reasons. The first is, I can't control someone else's fear of me. There have been situations, especially with police, in which I have felt the other person is on edge simply because I'm a black man. I don't want to give a person, or police officer with a gun, any reason to threaten me or shoot me. In my community, it's been proven that I'm more likely to get stopped by police than a white person is. I told Hayes about the statistics and science I have found to prove that blacks have good reason to fear for their safety when dealing with police.

I expected Hayes to push back on these points. Many middle-aged white men have done that when I presented these facts. But he didn't. In fact, he showed a striking measure of compassion. He acknowledged that we live in a time where black men feel targeted by police because of the color of their skin. That this intense climate exists, and that it is hard for him to fully understand what that feels like. Turns out, Hayes already had a similar conversation with a close friend of his who is a black man.

"We talked about this a lot. I had a belief that as long as you're doing the right thing and being respectful and being compliant, things that I know he would do if pulled over by the police, you'd be OK. But he just beat it into my head: 'Let me tell you something, it's different.' He said, 'I might be dressed nice and my hands are at ten and two and I'm scared to death the entire time I'm talking to a police officer that I'm going to give him some reason to shoot me.' I've never reacted that way to a police officer. I can't understand that, but I do have to understand that that's the way some people feel. I think it is reasonable to be concerned about that."

Still, Hayes believes that the only way forward in a situation like that, as a black man, is to do everything you're asked to do. At the end of the day, the person that you're dealing with has a gun. You don't. "I don't like governmental authority. I don't like being told what to do. But I don't like getting shot."

But what if the worst should happen? What if a black man was the person with the gun who shot the unarmed white man because he felt the white man had threatened his life? What happens then?

"I think you just have to know that you have the right to defend yourself, regardless of what anyone would tell you. If it's reasonable for you to assume that the person is going to hurt you — serious bodily injury is what the statue says — then you could and should use a gun to defend yourself. There's not supposed to be any racial bias in the court. But we know that sometimes there is. It could go either way."

No, no, it couldn't.

12

THE RAZOR'S EDGE

I STOPPED MY truck outside the Warren Theatre in Broken Arrow, so Lizzie could walk inside to print out our tickets from the kiosk while I roamed the crowded parking lot, looking for a good spot. It was just four days before Christmas. I was excited. We were going to see *Assassin's Creed,* a movie damn near tailored for me, and the kind Lizzie would never see if not for me.

I drove up and down, annoyed by all the people who seemed to have the same idea — to see a movie on a Wednesday night. I ended up parking near the deep end of the parking lot and hiking back to the entrance. By the time I'd stepped inside, Lizzie was ready and waiting for me. I felt good. I felt like me, in my black-and-red Sho'nuff hoodie, gray sweatpants, and brand-new Ohio State red LeBron Soldier Activations on my feet. Lizzie took my arm as we headed toward the ticket taker. Just as we got there, I was stopped. The sheriff's deputy approached me.

"Could I have a look inside your bag?"

My bag was a dopp kit, a faux-leather toiletry bag. It held my wallet, keys, phone, headphones, notebook, and pens. It was so small, I carried it on top of my forearm. Yet in this sea of white faces, even while standing next to a woman with a purse large enough to carry an inflated beach ball, the deputy chose me. He took a step forward and asked again to look inside my dopp kit. Just as I was about to unzip my bag for him, he spoke again.

"There are no weapons inside, right?"

"Just keys, man."

I unzipped my bag and rooted through my belongings for him. This was a Terry stop — a stop and frisk. The term comes from the 1968 US Supreme Court case Terry v. Ohio. John Terry had been searched by a police officer after the officer believed he saw Terry casing a store for a robbery. The court held that a police officer could search for weapons without a warrant, probable cause, when the officer reasonably believes that the person may be armed and dangerous.

Satisfied, the sheriff's deputy motioned for Lizzie and me to be on our way. Once we got past the ticket taker, I could feel my wife's embarrassment, confusion, and pain.

"I don't want to talk about it," I said.

"I did the right thing, though? I didn't lose my shit."

I squeezed her hand, and we headed into the movie. Even before the previews aired, I saw Lizzie was still in pain for me, and I pleaded with her to go to the bathroom and cry it out. When she returned, she seemed better. I thought I was fine too. I thought I could let go of this little tragedy, this small horror, like I had so many times before. Then, without warning, I was awash in my own tornado of furies. I tried to reckon with myself, but soon I told Lizzie I was heading to the bathroom. She knew I never do that during a movie. Walking the corridors outside the screening rooms, I couldn't bring myself to walk back in to watch the movie. Even knowing I was not the only black man to suffer these miniature atrocities, and that I would have to suffer many more to come, I couldn't wipe this one away. I called Lizzie from outside the theater and got her voicemail. But she knew me. She knew enough to know I was outside waiting for her. And there she came.

"Can we go?" I said.

"Yes. We can."

When we arrived back at our apartment, I asked Lizzie to leave me alone in the truck for a while.

"You want to take a walk?" she asked.

"Yes."

She left me to go inside. When I saw her disappear through the front door, I let myself cry. This was not the first time I had cried because the world had treated Lizzie and me differently. Perhaps if it was just the outside world and not her family too, my marriage would not have ended.

THERE WERE FOURTEEN vehicles this Thanksgiving at Charles's house. Of those fourteen, five were trucks. One was an ATV. One was a Polaris RZR, a kind of hybrid of a go-kart and a four-wheeler in need of an attitude adjustment. All of them were parked tightly together, leaving only a way open to the storm shelter we've sometimes had cause to herd into after seeing a tornado's funnel descending upon us. A string of cow skulls hung from the only tree near the house, a tree Nancy won't let Charles cut down. A life-size bronze statue of a buck watches over it. Half a football field to the north lies a trough that Charles fills with corn to feed the bucks and does that pass through because he knows Nancy likes to see the deer. The rule is, you can't shoot any of the deer approaching the trough. This means Charles has to stand down with his rifle while continuing to fill the trough. This is a measure of love.

After five families tied together by marriage and blood exchanged introductions, Nancy asked aloud if we should say a prayer before eating. Three women yelled out *Yes!* in unison, like a forbidding Greek chorus. Then two more women called for Charles.

"What?" he said.

"We need to say grace."

"I need to get my computer." Which is an iPad, but no matter how many times you tell him that, it's still a computer.

"Why?"

"Because I looked up prayers on it."

With his iPad in hand, Charles marched to the center of the gathering and began to read aloud. Like soldiers who know the drill, everyone bowed their heads, grabbed one another's hands, and filled the room with a silence that didn't enfold me so much as squeeze me. God has no place in my worldview because, if there was one, She wouldn't stand for the world I live in.

"That was a good prayer."

"Yeah, you need to print that out and give it to everybody."

"I haven't figured that out yet." Charles's unapologetic honesty was met with laughs while we began our ritual consumption of food on a secular holiday created to mythologize Pilgrims.

I'd promised Lizzie I'd avoid picking fights or taking undue offense at the things often said at these holiday dinners. Trying to keep this promise, I secluded myself in front of the living room TV, where football was on, and I was alone. I ate my meal in silence while trying to concentrate on the game. I knew if I dwelled on some of the views I'd heard expressed here, I would not be able to prevent myself from confronting someone about something—about any of the things wrong with this situation.

Two of the youngest of the clan came sprinting to a stop in front of me during the third quarter of the Detroit Lions–Minnesota Vikings game. The Vikings were driving, as Minnesota's running back Jerrick McKinnon, a muscular black man, caught a short swing pass and turned it into a big gain, planting the Vikings firmly inside the Lions' twenty-yard line. The boys were just old enough to be Webelo Scouts. Each held identical Nerf guns, like a sci-fi writer's idea of what revolvers will look like in two hundred years.

Then they pointed them at me.

"We're going to use you as target practice," one said.

"Yeah!" the other said.

In that moment, I decided they couldn't yet comprehend the meaning of pointing a gun of any kind at an unarmed black person and uttering those words, in that order, with that authoritative tone. They couldn't yet know how badly they'd hurt me.

"No, you won't," I said.

The words came out angrier, louder than I'd heard them in my head. The boys scurried away just as I realized I had turned into another angry black man. Then I tried to remember a time when I was not angry. The Vikings settled for a field goal, and the game continued.

NANCY HAS A need to send everyone she loves a Christmas card, and those cards thrust my very being into high relief. Such was the case when I tried to sneak away one Thanksgiving before Nancy caught me.

"We have to take the Christmas-card picture before you go."

I tried to hide my disgust, but I doubt I succeeded. Nancy retrieved for me one of the five matching shirts she plans for every year for her Christmas cards. This year Charles, Nancy, Jimmy, Lizzie, and I were all to wear a black sweatshirt with an illustration of Darth Vader wearing a Santa beanie, with the caption I FIND YOUR LACK OF CHEER

DISTURBING. I handed my phone to a relative to take this picture, at Nancy's request. He took it. And now there's another picture in which I stand in the middle of four white people, who are smiling into a sun unobscured by clouds during the last vestiges of fall. I showed this photograph to my dear friend Kate. She broke into a giggle fit when she realized what was in front of her. "One of these is not like the other," she said.

IN OUR TIME together, I believe Charles gained a greater understanding of what guns and gun ownership mean to me. He came to understand why it was more dangerous for me to carry a gun than it was for him — no matter how skilled and careful I am with one. I've watched him engage his friends in conversations about the shooting of unarmed black men in a way that is knowledgeable and forthright and built on the foundation of discussions he's had with me.

He no longer wonders aloud if an unarmed black man deserved to be shot by police, or if the unarmed black man was guilty of anything other than being in the wrong place at the wrong time. He's more critical of local law enforcement and its use of deadly force. He's empathetic and thoughtful about the black community's relationship with our fetid criminal justice system, and he has softened his stance on gun control. Over dinner one day, having seen his thinking slowly evolve, I told him I was proud of him. "Well, I care about my son-in-law," he said.

This was before he became so angry with me that he stole my jar of change when he helped Lizzie move out. This was just a month before his daughter and I got divorced.

LIZZIE AND I used to play a game when we went out in our hometown. We played the game whether we were seeing a movie at the Warren in Broken Arrow or eating pizza at Andolini's on Cherry Street or watching Jason Isbell sing at a concert at Cain's or sitting in the audience at the University of Tulsa to hear any one of the amazing artists the college brings in to speak. To play the game, we looked around the room, and we counted. We counted how many black people were in the room. To get a valid number, we excluded wait staff and event staff from the count. If the number reached double digits, we celebrated. But frequently in my hometown, and most other towns in Oklahoma we've lived in and visited, we didn't get to celebrate very often. Many times, I'm the only person who looks like me in the room. In those moments I don't want to go out again at all.

Lizzie and I used to play another game when we were out. This one, like the first, relied heavily on skin color but not so much on numbers. Whenever we saw an interracial couple, we'd approach them. We'd approach them, and then high-five them. We never once had to explain to the couple why we were high-fiving. We never once were met with anything other than excitement. I've never had to explain to an interracial couple the sinking feeling I had when Lizzie introduced me to one of her friends at law school. I'll call her Marie Antoinette because she was white, glowed with privilege and jewelry, and was eating cake at the time. I watched her contort her face and say, "Oh, I didn't know you were black." As if my ethnicity should have any bearing on whether or not I was her friend's husband. As if it mattered.

And then I realized, to her, it did. I didn't realize whiteness or blackness mattered to Lizzie either, until the days just prior to the 2016 presidential election, when my country chose to show its true face, as bigotry stood at the doorstep and opened the door wide. I didn't realize until too late that this is how a previously happy marriage comes to an end. I was pissed, and I was upset and venting more than a brick chimney at the height of the industrial revolution. I was so angry, yet I felt so safe with her, that I yelled out, "I *hate* white people!"

"But *I'm* white!"

A thing that had never dawned on me until she said it. I guess it had. But not in this way. Not connected to the visceral physicality those words evoked. In fact, the knowledge of her not being white but associating herself with *being* white felt like a rebuke. Because I thought of her as Lizzie, my wife. Not a white person, not a white woman, not my white wife — just Lizzie my wife. It felt as if, in that moment, I had no idea who I had married. I was no longer part of a single entity with this person I was supposed to share the rest of my life with. I felt hurt and dismayed and confused — so utterly confused.

All at once I felt horrifically scared too, utterly alone in this space, this apartment, where I had believed beyond doubt that the plights, tragedies, and insanities of the world could not get in.

The work I had done to get to know Lizzie's family had seemingly been for nothing. The postracial society I was striving to be a part of in coming to understanding Charles, and his effort to understand me, looked like an elaborate hoax because of the force Lizzie put on that word — *white*. The tears that streamed down her cheeks looked warm enough to burn, to scorch me with their honesty. In the games we had played, I wondered now whether the two of us ever had the same reasons for high-fiving other interracial couples. Were we counting the black people in the room for the same reasons? And there was the way Lizzie saw me, the way she'd seen me for years — the way I have been since I was a small child. I have been angry at the world. I have been devastated by it in such a manner, in such a violent rage with it, that I was blinded. I could not see how my seething had affected her. I realized that this razor's edge we'd been living on had not only begun to cut us, but had cut through us. Over the course of our marriage, that razor had been separating us into two individual parts that could no longer exist together. Admitting this was painful. It still is.

13

·················
·················
·················
·················
·················

SHOOTING WITH MOM

I DID NOT speak to my mother for a year after Lizzie and I decided to divorce. The rhetoric and emotion of the 2016 presidential election not only tore a schism in my marriage but also created a deeper divide within my family — the only one I had left. But now my pending divorce pushed me to seek out my mama. I wanted to be friends with her again. I needed family. But this wasn't going to be easy.

I am a very blue Democrat. My mother is a very red Republican. This makes her somewhat of a unicorn. How many black women decorate their black Ford F-150 with an American-flag magnet the size of a dinner platter and paste an NRA Lifetime Member sticker on the passenger side corner of the rearview mirror, just opposite a gold sticker with a capital T underlined and the slogan TRUMP FOR PRESIDENT? Out of that subset, how many black women conceal-carry not just one but two pistols every time they go out? Like I said, my mother is something of a unicorn.

Grandmomme, whom I called most Tuesdays, confessed she could talk to her youngest child only if the conversation didn't involve politics. "I told her I'm not fooling with that mess," Grandmomme said.

I hadn't yet told my mother about my pending divorce, and I wasn't sure I was ready to. But I figured it was time to see if she even cared to know me anymore. If anything had changed with her. If there was some way we could be family again without ending our meetings with shouting matches and hurt feelings. I wanted to see if I could hear her. I wanted to believe she could hear me.

My mom was enthusiastic just to have me call. When I asked her if she would like to meet me right then for pizza, her only thought was whether she was dressed appropriately. When I picked her up from the pharmacy where she'd gone to retrieve her purse — she'd left it there while filling a prescription — I saw immediately how much this woman, turning sixty that year, had changed physically. And how she was still the exuberant and defiant woman who had raised me. In my truck, driving to Andolini's, we tried to make small talk.

"Your truck runs smooth," she said.

"Thanks, Ma."

"How many miles on it?"

"Just over a hundred thousand."

"Runs smooth."

I told her I had to take care of it. It's the only truck I got. Not long after this, she volunteered that her truck payment was $400 a month, and she was thinking about downsizing to a car. "I don't need something so big anymore," she said. I tried to make the small talk last a little longer, but it didn't take. I came out with the news about my divorce, and my mother was hurt. This Christian woman had been married to my father for over thirty years. She couldn't fathom how Lizzie and I had let it come to this; how we were so ready to let each other go, without putting up what she thought was a necessary fight to save our marriage.

She was still going on about it when I came around the truck to help her out, and she wrapped her hand around my bicep. This was a gesture she'd performed in the past, but this time I felt the full weight of her. When she asked me to slow down as we were going through the crosswalk, I realized my mother was so frail now, she needed me to hold her up to walk across the street.

When we sat down to order, we began to talk about what I was up to. But I was stuck on the fact that this woman in front of me was speaking slower, moving slower, even though I knew she'd been on disability after suffering a back injury while working at a call center years back, a job she took on because she could not make the money she once had as an alcohol and drug counselor. I took stock of the bulge at her hip and the bulge in the small of her back, under her blue cardigan and hidden from view for anyone untrained to look for such things. When I pointed out she was carrying, my mother shushed me. I was not surprised I was shushed. I was surprised she carried a gun. She had white

Converse sneakers on her feet. Her naked shins led to blue capris. The salt-and-pepper hair spurting from beneath her TU ball cap made her the picture of a gentle brown grandmother. Ruin and woe to the person who didn't realize my mama was strapped and looking for an excuse.

MY MOTHER HAS a master's in marriage and family therapy from the University of Southern Mississippi. Her office was at Pine Grove Behavioral Health and Addiction Services in Hattiesburg. At Pine Grove, my mother thrived. I knew this because at that time my sister and I were in her back pocket.

She took us everywhere with her. She introduced us to everyone. I remember running the halls of the rehab facility. Building forts out of plush cushions in waiting areas. Playing Ping-Pong with recovering addicts who insisted on playing for something. I'd put up my Capri Sun against their cigarettes. Whether they let me win or I was just that good is open to debate. What's true is that the packs of cigarettes ended up in the trash, much to the chagrin of the folks who thought I'd be a good sport and give back the cigarettes they knew Mom wouldn't let us smoke. This was the only environment I've known in which race simply wasn't spoken about or thrown back in my face in a way that hurt. I never knew how much that meant until I was a teenager in very white, very conservative Oklahoma.

Our moving from Mississippi to Florida when I was ten and then to Oklahoma when I was thirteen meant that my mother's professional license to practice was no longer valid. For a time, she worked for the Department of Children and Families in Panama City, Florida, as a social worker. She was trying so hard to be the kind of woman who could continue to work full-time and raise two young children. But the work was uninteresting and everlasting. My mother was tired, and couldn't help me as much with schoolwork, so I began to suffer in my overwhelmed school. I didn't care so much to study anymore. So my mother made a decision.

She resolved to home-school Denise and me. That's how I went through seventh and eighth grade. By the time we moved again, to Tulsa, following my father's job, I was beginning to see that my parents had made some wrong choices, pursued the wrong opportunities. My father didn't have a college degree then, and when, because of this, he was continually passed over for a better position, he took offense and ultimately quit. This led to bitterness, and to my decision to leave for college and never return. In keeping that promise to myself, though, I lost my parents. My parents lost me.

OUR SERVER TOOK our order. Ma ordered sweet iced tea. I ordered unsweetened iced tea, and the server left us to look over the menu.

"Still watching your figure?" Ma said.

"Clearly not. I'm about to order a pepperoni pizza."

She smiled. "You do that every time you come here?"

"I know what I like."

"Well, I'm going to be a little more adventurous."

Ma ended up ordering all the fixings. Something she wasn't going to finish and wouldn't take home. I pointed that out to her.

"You'll finish it," she said.

"No, Ma. I won't."

"See? Watching your figure."

A lull set in, and Ma looked at me expectantly. Like I should ask her something. So I asked her when she'd bought her gun and why.

"I got my first gun August 26 of 2012," my mom said, "and joined the NRA. Joined the USCCA." While I was coming to the end of my gun odyssey, deciding I wouldn't shoot anymore because I didn't believe the world would be a better place with me preparing to shoot back, my mother, I was just now discovering, had begun her own.

She was scared. That's what she said. She said she was scared, and she wasn't going to allow herself to be a victim in a world she saw growing madder by the day. Mom got a gun a month after James Holmes killed twelve people at the Century 16 movie theater in Aurora, Colorado.

"I like to go to the movies," Ma said. "Least I used to. Then the Colorado shoot-up thing happened. And all those people sitting in the movie theater — he was just killing them all. And loading some more. And killing more. I said, 'I ain't going out like that.' Since then I've had a number of things reinforce that viewpoint."

One gun wasn't enough, though. The news she consumed

had informed her of that. This is a woman who cleaned her house to the sound of Rush Limbaugh blaring from her phone, who believed Glenn Beck was a saint until "he started to move to the left," who denounced Megyn Kelly as traitorous because she called Donald Trump on his bullshit, and who doesn't understand why many of us don't like Trump.

"Why do you like Donald Trump though, Ma?"

"RJ, he's saying all the things I feel."

"So we need a wall?"

"To keep the drugs and Mexican criminals out, yeah."

"A wall, Mom?"

"The Chinese have had one to keep the rest of the world out for centuries. Why is it a big deal that we want to build one too?"

I changed the subject. "You still shoot regularly?" Making conversation now, believing this to be an easy segue.

"I would shoot practically every day of the week," she said. "Now it's a little harder for me to get around. I need to get back to it. You still shoot like you did?"

"No, Ma."

"Shame. You're a good shot."

"Doesn't matter."

"You told me the last time we talked that you don't carry a gun. I hope you never get into a situation where you have to change your mind."

Our server came back with pizzas. Ma was taken aback at the size of her fourteen-inch pie.

"Goodness gracious. I'm never gonna finish this." Then she looked up at me again.

"I've got all I can handle in front of me."

Ma frowned and began to dig into her pizza. She looked up at me, briefly. Then looked back down at her pizza. I waited for whatever it was she looked like she was bursting to say. Her face showed a vulnerability I hadn't seen in years. Her lip quivered just a bit. I could feel her waiting for me to say something — anything. But not a whole lot came.

A FEW WEEKS later my mother called me.

"I haven't been able to figure out why I'm falling off to the right of my shot," she said, "and it was making me mad. Then I remembered my son is a certified pistol instructor. You think you could help me?"

"I don't shoot anymore, Mom." I knew she remembered that too. At that point, I hadn't gone to a gun range in months.

"Who said anything about *you* shooting? This is about *me*."

I sighed. But then it occurred to me that this was my mother at her most humble. Over lunch I had learned that her favorite hobby now was shooting her pistols, and that she took great pride in being a good marksman. It was a source of immense satisfaction that I, her son, am a better shot than she is and of great consternation that I didn't care to shoot anymore. "Can you go Sunday afternoon?"

I met my mother at her apartment complex with my

range bag in hand, as she was using a dolly to ferry her gear to her truck. Her bag was twice the size of mine, and she was bringing two different kinds of targets. The white-and-gold MAKE AMERICA GREAT AGAIN hat atop her head completed the look. She waved at me.

"Hey, Bud!"

I jogged up to her and pulled her range bag off the cart, threw it across my free shoulder, and carried both items to her truck. She took much longer than she would've liked to climb into her truck, muttering about how she needed something smaller. Then she turned over the engine. Before pulling out of the parking lot, she shot me a look.

"You bring your NRA instructor hat?" she said.

"It's in the bag."

"Good. I want these folks to see that."

We were a sight when we pulled into the United States Shooting Academy parking lot — which is right next door to the Tulsa Police Department. I was in sweatpants, a hoodie, and Jordans, and had my NRA instructor hat on backward. My mother looked very much at home in this lobby filled with handguns, shotguns, and rifles of all stripes. I filled out the Academy paperwork and left my driver's license as collateral. Mom then drove us to an open shooting bay. While she was taking her favored full-size FNS-9 pistol out of the bag, she made the mistake of lifting it so the gun barrel was pointed at me. I swerved out of range.

"If you point that at me again, we're getting in the truck and going home," I said. "You know better."

My mother looked like she'd been scolded for neglecting to clean her room. "Sorry."

After that, we quickly fell into a teacher-student relationship as I put my mother through my usual warm-up of shooting twenty-one shots from close range to ten yards away. I was struck by how willing she was to do exactly what I asked without the slightest hesitation.

Occasionally, she would question why we were doing an exercise. Once she discovered the reasoning, though, she went back to listening. This willingness to be patient, to be teachable, had also emerged in me over the several years I'd spent learning to get good with a gun. Now I realized where that came from. After all, my mother was my first teacher.

When I showed her how she was rushing, how she wouldn't allow herself to relax before firing, and the steps to correct the problem, she started hitting the bull's-eye. In fact, she started hitting it at such a consistent clip, she wanted to have a brief match with me.

"This is your lesson, Mom. Not mine."

"So?"

"I haven't shot in months."

"You scared you're gonna lose?"

"Fine."

I set the rules. From twenty yards out, we would each get to take three shots at tiny targets. Closest grouping wins. My mother shot first. Whether she was flustered or instantly forgot what I had taught her, she went high and right with her first shot. Then she barely clipped the target with the second. She was an inch away from the bull's-eye with the third.

"OK," I said. "My turn. If my first two hit inside the target, I win. No need for a third, right?"

"Cocky, aren't you?"

I put three rounds in my magazine, loaded into my Glock, and took two deep breaths. I let off two shots in rapid succession.

"You missed with the second," Mom said.

"No, I didn't. Check."

We locked the slide back on each of our pistols, and laid them on the table. Then we walked to the target. My mother let her fingers search the target.

"*Damn.*" I'd put two holes right next to each other in the center of the target. "My son can *shoot.*" She pulled me close, hugged me, and kissed my cheek. She let go then and pulled back, with a sheepish look. She almost whispered the words: "You want to try to be friends again?"

14

HANDS UP

I WAS ALWAYS aware of the irony of relying on guns to try to get close to my white father-in-law. Just as I am aware of the irony of spending a day at the gun range to begin to repair my relationship with Mom.

But I make no apology for using anything at hand to get closer to another human being. I never will.

If I've learned anything during my odyssey into guns and their role in our country, it's that we are in a literal arms race, ramped up by the racialized fear peddled to us by damn near every institutionalized force in the land. Gun culture in America is inherently racist because white people historically fear black men with guns. I have cited facts, history, story, and policy to prove this point. And yet I live as a black man in a country where too many people are so afraid of being called racist that they will not confront their own racism — around guns, around their social, economic, or constitutional privilege.

I wrote this book because I wanted to understand not only Charles, but the people — mostly white people — who feel they must carry a gun for self-protection. I wanted to know who they felt they needed protection from. I wanted to demonstrate my willingness to reach out to them.

My odyssey taught me a great deal about the escalating cycles of white fear that fuel black fear and the insanity of American gun culture. My odyssey did not teach me how to be a man without being a black man first. And has made me more afraid for my life than ever before.

My letter to white people would begin by asking you to speak up for me. When you are in a room full of other white folks who are making insensitive or coded or hateful remarks about those of us who are not white, you are the only voice we have. If you are not heard, then we are silenced. That frightens me. But it does not frighten me as much as the task of convincing you that the way forward is for you to feel uncomfortable. You have to step into the fire with me, to feel that distress and pain and anguish. Because I will never live safely in the world without the sacrifices of those whose birth certificates and driver's licenses say this: white.

I am expert with a handgun. Yet both of my guns remain unloaded and stored in a cool, dry place where a padlock has final say over who can get to them. This is because I understand the historical significance of a black man owning a gun in his home. I understand why it's important to guard my Second Amendment rights. I also understand that the Second Amendment — or my exercise of it — isn't going to stop misinformed and racist people from shooting and killing me because of how I fit into their biases. Only empathy will overcome that. Only an understanding that my life is valuable will shoot that down.

ACKNOWLEDGMENTS

Thank you, Lizzie Stafford, for loving me. Your intelligence and kindness sustained me.

Thank you, Mama and Papa. What we've gone through just proves our love.

Thank you, Ron Taylor. You are the brother I always wanted. Thank you too, Yolanda Taylor, for a safe place. And thank you, Ron Taylor Sr., for lifting me up and dusting me off.

Thank you dearly, Charles Stafford and Nancy Stafford. You never blinked at welcoming me and loving me.

Thank you, Mary Wafer-Johnston, for loving me when I did not love myself.

Thank you, Laurel Williamson, for the bread and water.

Thank you, Weapon X and Brave. I've only ever been RJ to you.

Thank you, Tyler Burroughs, for not allowing me to spend New Year's Day alone.

Thank you, Kate Galatian, for being my Lasso of Truth.

Thank you, Celia Ampel, for your patience as a reader and a listener.

Chris Lusk, you have my gratitude for being the first editor who gave a damn.

Thank you, Sarah Szabo, my favorite superhero.

Thank you, Katy Mullins, for calling until I picked up.

Thank you, Dr. Amber Coyle McConnell, for teaching me to swim through pain.

I want to express heartfelt appreciation to my agent, Michelle Tessler. Also to Deanne Urmy, my editor at Houghton Mifflin Harcourt, for believing in me.

NOTES

2. WE'RE ALL MAD HERE

page

14   *one in six black men in prison:* Ashley Nellis, "The Color of Justice: Racial and Ethnic Disparities in State Prisons," in *The Sentencing Project,* June 14, 2016. http://www.sentencingproject.org/publica tions/color-of-justice-racial-and-ethnic-disparity-in-state-pris ons/#II. Overall Findings.

15   *40 goddamn percent:* Ibid.

3. GLOCK

29   *literally laughed at him:* Paul M. Barrett, *GLOCK: The Rise of America's Gun* (New York: Crown Publishers, 2012), p. 7.

30   *"I should fire ten thousand rounds":* Ibid., p. 11.
     It was his seventeenth invention: Ibid., p. 13.

31   *"Five thousand miles":* Peter G. Kokalis, "Plastic Perfection," in *Soldier of Fortune,* October 1984. https://remtek.com/arms/glock/ model/9/17/index.html

32   *"Gaddafi Buying Austrian":* Barrett, *Glock,* p. 40.
     "Hijacker's Special": Ibid., p. 41.
     "an edge that officials": Ibid., p. 43.
     "super gun": Ibid., p. 63.

4. OBAMA AIN'T GONNA KNOW

38   *right in line with the national:* "995 People Shot Dead in 2015,"
      Washington Post, June 30, 2016. https://www.washingtonpost.com/
      graphics/national/police-shootings/
      more than two thousand gun shows: The Bureau of Alcohol, To-
      bacco, Firearms and Explosives, "The Bureau of Alcohol, Tobacco,
      Firearms and Explosives' Investigative Operations at Gun Shows,"
      June 2007. https://oig.justice.gov/reports/ATF/e0707/final.pdf

39   *Wanenmacher's was sponsored:* Kelly Bostian, "Wanenmacher Arms
      Show Marks 60 Years in Guns, Politics, Celebrities," *Tulsa World,*
      November 8, 2014. http://www.tulsaworld.com/newshomepage1/
      wanenmacher-arms-show-marks-years-in-guns-politics-celebrities/
      article_268aac76-1bb7-569f-9c67-dc7cad0965f1.html
      Wanenmacher counted 117 tables: Doug Howlett, "The Gun Digest
      Interview: Joe Wanenmacher," *Gun Digest,* May 3, 2013. https://gun
      digest.com/reviews/the-gun-digest-interview-joe-wanenmacher

41   *"Our good president probably":* Bostian, "Wanenmacher Arms Show."

43   *92 percent of Americans:* Sarah Dutton, Jennifer De Pinto, Anthony
      Salvanto, and Fred Backus, "CBS/NYT Poll: GOP Voters Have Deep
      Concern About Government," CBS News, October 27, 2015. https://
      www.cbsnews.com/news/cbsnyt-poll-gop-voters-have-deep-con
      cerns-about-government/
      Over 9 million guns: Tiffany Hsu, "How Many Guns Sold? Why It's
      Hard to Tell," *New York Times,* March 3, 2018. https://www.nytimes.
      com/2018/03/02/business/gun-sales-impact.html

44   *states have established laws:* Giffords Law Center, "Universal
      Background Checks," June 2017. http://lawcenter.giffords.org/
      gun-laws/policy-areas/background-checks/universal-background-
      checks/

45   *flyer being circulated around:* Dylan Goforth and Kassie McClung,
      "Two Racist Incidents at OU Following Trump Election Among
      Handful Reported in Oklahoma," *The Frontier,* November 14, 2016.
      https://www.readfrontier.org/stories/racist-incidents-at-ou-post-
      election-among-several-reported-in-state/

5. GRANDMOMME

49   *"black men are more capable":* John Wilson, PhD, Montclair University; Kurt Hugenberg, PhD, Miami University; and Nicholas Rule, PhD, University of Toronto, "Racial Bias in Judgments of Physical Size and Formidability: From Size to Threat," *Journal of Personality and Social Psychology,* published online March 13, 2017. https://www.apa.org/pubs/journals/releases/psp-pspi0000092.pdf

50   *460 people who died:* Jaeah Lee, "Here's the Data That Shows Cops Kill Black People at a Higher Rate Than White People," *Mother Jones,* September 10, 2014. http://www.motherjones.com/politics/2014/09/police-shootings-ferguson-race-data/
     "The lesson this teaches": Ida B. Wells, "Southern Horrors: Lynch Law in All Its Phases," *New York Age,* June 25, 1892.

52   *"I don't have to give you anything":* Adam Winkler, "The Secret History of Guns," *The Atlantic,* September 2011. https://www.theatlantic.com/magazine/archive/2011/09/the-secret-history-of-guns/308608/

53   *"The American people in general":* Ibid.

54   *"The supposed aim of this bill":* David Babat, "The Discriminatory History of Gun Control." Senior Honors Projects, Paper 140, May 2009. http://digitalcommons.uri.edu/srhonorsprog/140

6. THERE IS NO TRY

63   *Plaxico Burress rather famously:* Casey Glynn, "Ex–New York Giant Plaxico Burress Released from Prison Monday," Associated Press, June 6, 2011. https://www.cbsnews.com/news/ex-new-york-giant-plaxico-burress-released-from-prison-monday/

7. WALDO

71   *handgun license:* Michael McNutt, "Oklahoma Gov. Mary Fallin Signs Open-Carry Gun Bill into Law," *The Oklahoman,* May 15, 2012. http://newsok.com/article/3675750

8. WHITE NRA

81   *NRA Family website has published:* Linda Hoff, "Throwback
      Thursday: Davy Crockett," NRA Family, September 7, 2017.
      https://www.nrafamily.org/articles/2017/9/7/throwback-thursday-
      davy-crockett/.

83   *"included stories in which Crockett":* Laura Browder, *Slippery Char-*
      acters: Ethnic Impersonators and American Identities (Chapel Hill,
      North Carolina: University of North Carolina Press, 2006), p. 52.
      from these racist statements: David Crockett, *A Narrative Life of*
      David Crocket of the State of Tennessee (Philadelphia: E. L. Carey
      and A. Hart; Baltimore: Carey, Hart & Co., University of California
      Libraries, 1834), p. 4.
      writings such as his pseudo-memoir: James Strange French,
      Sketches and Eccentricities of Col. David Crockett of West Tennessee
      (New York: J. & J. Harper, The Library of Congress, 1833).

84   *May 21, 1997, was the day:* Joel Achenbach, Scott Higham, and Sari
      Horwitz, "How NRA's True Believers Converted a Marksmanship
      Group into a Mighty Gun Lobby," *Washington Post,* January 12, 2013.
      https://www.washingtonpost.com/politics/how-nras-true-believers-
      converted-a-marksmanship-group-into-a-mighty-gun-lobby/2013
      /01/12/51c62288-59b9-11e2-88d0-c4cf65c3ad15_story.html?utm_
      term=.9de79217a694.

85   *its now infamous super PAC:* British Broadcasting Corporation,
      "US Gun Control: What Is the NRA and Why Is It So Powerful?"
      January 8, 2016. http://www.bbc.com/news/world-us-canada-
      35261394
      Frederick testified before Congress: Adam Winkler, "NRA Took a
      Hard Right After Leadership Coup," *San Francisco Chronicle,* July 28,
      2012. http://www.sfgate.com/opinion/article/NRA-took-hard-right-
      after-leadership-coup-3741640.php

86   *40 million in 1970:* Adam Winkler, "The NRA Will Fall. It's Inevi-
      table," *Washington Post,* October 19, 2015. https://www.washing
      tonpost.com/posteverything/wp/2015/10/19/the-nra-will-fall-its-
      inevitable/?utm_term=.7b2f3d94321d

87   *Robert Corbin invoked the Alamo:* Michael Isikoff, "NRA Leaders
      Vow All-Out Fight Against 'Brady Bill,'" *Washington Post,* April 14,

1991. https://www.washingtonpost.com/archive/politics/1991/04/14/
nra-leaders-vow-all-out-fight-against-brady-bill/37a01994-d1a4-
4b31-9e52-40a999efd5d9/?utm_term=.135728422a12.

NRA declared more than $227 million: Dan Bigman, "What the
NRA's Wayne LaPierre Gets Paid to Defend Guns, *Forbes,* December
21, 2012. https://www.forbes.com/sites/danbig
man/2012/12/21/what-the-nras-wayne-lapierre-gets-paid-to-defend-
guns/#5ca9912116d6

88 *"We must declare that there":* Wayne LaPierre, "2002 NRA Annual Meeting Speech by Wayne LaPierre," NRA-ILA, May 1, 2002.
https://www.nraila.org/articles/20020501/2002-nra-annual-meet
ing-speech-by-wayne-lapierre

2016 Pew Research Center poll: Pew Research Center, "Public Views About Guns," June 22, 2017. http://www.people-press.
org/2017/06/22/public-views-about-guns/#race.

Some cities have experienced: Adam Winkler, *Gun Fight: The Battle
over the Right to Bear Arms in America* (New York City: W.W. Norton
& Company, 2013).

9. BLACK NRA

91 *police officer Jeronimo Yanez:* T. Rees Shapiro, Lindsey Bever, Wes-
ley Lowery, and Michael E. Miller, "Police Group: Minn. Governor
'Exploited What Was Already a Horrible and Tragic Situation,'"
Washington Post, July 9, 2016. https://www.washingtonpost.com/
news/morning-mix/wp/2016/07/07/minn-cop-fatally-shoots-
man-during-traffic-stop-aftermath-broadcast-on-facebook/?utm_
term=.285fafa4ecda

92 *the NRA took its time:* Brian Fung, "The NRA's Internal Split over
Philando Castile," *Washington Post,* July 9, 2016. https://www.
washingtonpost.com/news/post-nation/wp/2016/07/09/the-nras-
internal-revolt-over-philando-castile/?utm_term=.97bf633d35b5

93 *They use media to assassinate:* Dana Loesch, "Freedom's Safest
Place: The Violence of Lies," NRA, April 7, 2017. https://www.you
tube.com/watch?v=XtGOQFf9VCE

94 *documented 867 incidents:* SPLC, "Ten Days After: Harassment and
Intimidation in the Aftermath of the Election," Southern Poverty
Law Center, November 29, 2016. http://www.politifact.com/texas/

statements/2012/oct/05/stefani-carter/stefani-carter-says-black-women-texas-fastest-grow/

95 *Don't let your kids":* Ted Nugent, Facebook, November 24, 2014. https://www.facebook.com/tednugent/posts/10152535118862297.

96 *In a photo for the* Los Angeles Times: Molly Hennessey-Fiske, "NRA's Black Commentator Becomes Web Sensation," *Los Angeles Times,* July 23, 2013. http://www.latimes.com/nation/la-na-black-guns-nra-20130723-dto-htmlstory.html

97 *group reach membership of 250,000:* Paxton Delaney, "Celebrating the National African American Gun Association's One-Year Anniversary," NRABlog, March 22, 2016. https://www.nrablog.com/articles/2016/3/celebrating-the-national-african-american-gun-associations-one-year-anniversary/
hadn't even been introduced to guns: Ibid.
"The only time I saw a gun": Ibid.
"Our organization is working hard": Ibid.
NAAGA's membership saw a jump: Ryan Young, "African-American Gun Club Says Membership Surged in Trump Era," CNN, February 27, 2017. http://www.cnn.com/2017/02/27/us/african-american-gun-club-trump/index.html
"There's nothing hidden": Jake Dubois, "Black NAAGA: Are Guns Positive Thing For African Americans?" Black Lives Matter US, September 15, 2016. https://blackmattersus.com/15983-naaga-are-guns-positive-thing-for-african-americans/

98 *"A lot of African American gun owners":* Paxton Delaney, "Celebrating." *NRAblog,* March 22, 2016, https://www.nrablog.com/articles/2016/3/celebrating-the-national-african-american-gun-associations-one-year-anniversary/
"I'd be lying to you": Keith Whitney, "Group Training African-Americans to Use Guns Seeing Spike in Membership," CBS 46, May 30, 2017. http://www.cbs46.com/story/35300674/group-training-african-americans-to-use-guns-seeing-spike-in-membership

104 *black women were murdered:* Stefani Carter, "Stefani Carter Says Black Women are Texas' Fastest-Growing Group of Concealed-Handgun Permit Applicants," Politifact, http://www.politifact.com/texas/statements/2012/oct/05/stefani-carter/stefani-carter-says-black-women-texas-fastest-grow/

"about a three- to four-fold": Trymaine Lee, "The Age of Trump Is Producing More Black Gun Owners," *NBC News,* May 12, 2017. https://www.nbcnews.com/news/nbcblk/age-trump-produc ing-more-black-gun-owners-n758211

106 *49 percent of white households:* Kim Parker, Juliana Menasce Horowitz, Ruth Igielnik, Baxter Oliphant, and Anna Brown, "America's Complex Relationship with Guns," Pew Research Center, June 22, 2017. http://www.pewsocialtrends.org/2017/06/22/americas-complex-relationship-with-guns/

10. YOU'RE WORTH MORE TO ME, ASSHOLE

107 *310 million guns in circulation:* Dave Gilson, "10 Pro-Gun Myths, Shot Down," *Mother Jones,* January 31, 2013. http://www.mother jones.com/politics/2013/01/pro-gun-myths-fact-check/

111 *a Kel-Tec 9 mm PF-9:* Orlando Sentinel, "Behind the Handgun George Zimmerman Used to Kill Trayvon Martin," *Orlando Sentinel,* May 15, 2012. http://jacksonville.com/news/crime/2012-05-15/story/behind-handgun-george-zimmerman-used-kill-trayvon-martin

11. SELF-DEFENSE IN BLACK AND WHITE

116 *Texas resident Joe Horn called:* Patrick Michels, "Joe Horn and Five Years with Texas Castle Doctrine," *Texas Observer,* May 8, 2012. http://www.texasobserver.org/joe-horn-and-castle-doctrine-shoot ings-in-texas/

119 *"This is basically preparing people":* Sara DiNatale, "Tampa Man Shoots Father of Three, Then Calls 'Stand Your Ground' Hotline," *Tampa Bay Times,* September 16, 2016. http://www.tampabay.com/news/publicsafety/crime/tampa-man-shoots-father-of-three-then-calls-stand-your-ground-hotline/2293853

122 *$130 a year for peace of mind:* Adam Weinstein, "The Texas Legal Outfit Accused of Preying on Concealed Carry Holders," *The Trace,* August 17, 2015. https://www.thetrace.org/2015/08/texas-law-shield-concealed-carry-insurance-class-action-lawsuit/.

123 *Brad Crowley v. Texas Law Shield:* Michael David Miller, "Brad Crowley and Terrilyn Crowley, on Behalf of Themselves and All

Others Similarly Situated v. Texas Law Shield, Llp, Darren R. Rice,
T. Edwin Walker, Walker & Rice, Pc, and Walker & Byington, Pllc,"
Texas 14th Court of Appeals, June 23, 2017. http://data.scotxblog.
com/scotx/no/17-0096
"any incident where the Legal Service": Mark Bennett, "2015.18:
Texas Law Shield and Second Call Defense," blog.bennettand
bennett.com, January 13, 2015. http://blog.bennettandbennett.
com/2015/01/2015-18-texas-law-shield-and-second-call-defense/

126 *Governor Mary Fallin signed:* Associated Press, "Fallin Signs Bill
Allowing Young Veterans to Carry Guns, US News, April 6, 2017
https://www.usnews.com/news/best-states/oklahoma/articles/
2017-04-06/fallin-signs-bill-allowing-young-veterans-to-carry-guns
"a concealed or unconcealed weapon": Oklahoma Title 21, "Unlawful
Carry in Certain Places," Enacted during the 2017 Oklahoma Legislative session. http://www.oscn.net/applications/oscn/DeliverDocu
ment.asp?CiteID=69745

128 *Zach Peters was asleep:* Kyle Hinchey, "Friends in Disbelief over
Deaths of Three Teens During Home-Invasion," *Tulsa World,* March
30, 2017. http://www.tulsaworld.com/news/crimewatch/friends-in-
disbelief-over-deaths-of-three-teens-during-home/article_d5cab1a8-
bbe2-5732-aef9-4ad58408e7a0.html
"OK, sir, we're getting": Kimberly Querry, "Listen: 911 Call Released After Homeowner Shoots Three Intruders in Oklahoma
Home," News 4 Channel KFOR, March 29, 2017. http://kfor.
com/2017/03/29/listen-911-call-released-after-homeowner-shoots-
three-intruders-in-oklahoma-home/

12. THE RAZOR'S EDGE

138 *The court held that a police officer:* Case Briefs, "Terry v. Ohio," 392
U.S. 1, 88 S. Ct. 1868, 20 L. Ed. 2d 889 (1968), casebriefs.com, January 20, 2018, date last accessed. https://www.casebriefs.com/blog/
law/criminal-procedure/criminal-procedure-keyed-to-weinreb/the-
fourth-amendment-arrest-and-search-and-seizure/terry-v-ohio-4/

INDEX